ROUTLEDGE LIBRARY EDITIONS: AUTOBIOGRAPHY

Volume 5

A HEALING ART: REGENERATION THROUGH AUTOBIOGRAPHY

A HEALING ART: REGENERATION THROUGH AUTOBIOGRAPHY

MARILYN CHANDLER MCENTYRE

Routledge
Taylor & Francis Group
LONDON AND NEW YORK

First published in 1990

This edition first published in 2016
by Routledge
2 Park Square, Milton Park, Abingdon, Oxon OX14 4RN

and by Routledge
711 Third Avenue, New York, NY 10017

Routledge is an imprint of the Taylor & Francis Group, an informa business

© 1990 Marilyn R. Chandler

All rights reserved. No part of this book may be reprinted or reproduced or utilised in any form or by any electronic, mechanical, or other means, now known or hereafter invented, including photocopying and recording, or in any information storage or retrieval system, without permission in writing from the publishers.

Trademark notice: Product or corporate names may be trademarks or registered trademarks, and are used only for identification and explanation without intent to infringe.

British Library Cataloguing in Publication Data
A catalogue record for this book is available from the British Library

ISBN: 978-1-138-93641-6 (Set)
ISBN: 978-1-315-67463-6 (Set) (ebk)
ISBN: 978-1-138-94117-5 (Volume 5) (hbk)
ISBN: 978-1-138-94196-0 (Volume 5) (pbk)
ISBN: 978-1-315-67383-7 (Volume 5) (ebk)

Publisher's Note
The publisher has gone to great lengths to ensure the quality of this reprint but points out that some imperfections in the original copies may be apparent.

Disclaimer
The publisher has made every effort to trace copyright holders and would welcome correspondence from those they have been unable to trace.

A HEALING ART
REGENERATION THROUGH AUTOBIOGRAPHY

Marilyn R. Chandler

GARLAND PUBLISHING
New York & London
1990

Copyright © 1990 by Marilyn R. Chandler
All Rights Reserved

Library of Congress Cataloging-in-Publication Data

Chandler, Marilyn R.
A healing art: regeneration through autobiography/ Marilyn R. Chandler.
p. cm.—(Garland studies in comparative literature)
Includes bibliographical references.
ISBN 0-8240-5999-9 (alk. paper)
1. Autobiographies. 2. Life change events—Psychological aspects.
I. Title. II. Series.
CT101.C38 1990
920—dc20 90-42087

Printed on acid-free, 250-year-life paper.
Manufactured in the United States of America

For Mary, Elizabeth, and Margaret
with love

ACKNOWLEDGEMENTS

Foucault was right to call authorship a cooperative enterprise. Certainly this book would never have been completed without the help of a number of people whose interest in my work and generosity toward me has been deeply gratifying. I owe particular thanks to each of those who read it in its earlier stages: Robert Fagles, who showed me how to read with a difference--and from the heart; Emory Elliott, who broadened my understanding of American literature and deepened my love for it; Ruth Angress, who by apporaching difficult things with sensitivity, humor, and compassion, helped me to find some of "the right questions"; and Bill Howarth, who showed me what joy there is in the "wrestle with words and meanings," taught me to honor facts and delight in metaphors, and encouraged me not to cease from exploration.

I also want to thank several friends who saw me through to the completion of the manuscript with unfailing charity, wit, and intelligent advice: Vicki Reback, who always makes me think again and look a little harder; Patricia and David Troxel, for friendship, good conversation, and salient criticism; Jane Fremon, whose enthusiasm so often renewed my own; Kathryn Reiss, who watched this labor with love and taught me much about healing; Tom Strychacz, who shared my carrel, read my drafts, and cared for me in the "uncertain hours" with simple good sense, with poetry, and sometimes with silence.

Finally I am most deeply grateful to five people without whose loving support I could not have arrived at this completion: Mary, Elizabeth, and Margaret, who believed I could do it, Fred, who understood why I wanted to, and Michael, who assures me this is only a beginning.

PREFACE

Many post-World War I autobiographies focus upon episodes of crisis. In a century torn by global strife and the breakdown of cultural institutions, autobiography provides a way of recovering from crisis and restructuring reality--a healing act, involving the writer in a "wrestle with words and meanings" that can be deeply regenerative. Narration is a way of purging guilt and pain, re-centering the self, and reconnecting with community after crisis has driven one into silence and isolation.

Certain literary problems are endemic to crisis narratives. The first is to find words for the "inexpressible." The strategies writers invent to "raid the inarticulate" are various, but the problem is common to victims of extremity. Solutions range from redefinition of terms by subversion to attempts to make silence an essential part of the text--to "speak silence," as Elie Wiesel has put it.

Narrative perspective is another crucial issue in autobiography considered as a healing act. The stance a writer assumes in relation to his or her past determines the efficacy of autobiography as a means of recovery. Healing may, in fact, be measured by the degree of authority, irony, and imaginative transformation the writer exercises upon the raw facts of experience. Self-examination and decision are an integral part of authorship for an autobiographer writing to emerge from crisis.

Form is a third crucial issue in crisis narratives. Like words, narrative structures tend to be governed by tradition and convention, and therefore to exclude or obliterate those experiences that do not lend themselves to conventional shaping. Narrative forms can, however, become symbols of wholeness, providing the author with a gestalt that allows him or her to see the experience from "outside." Borrowing paradigms from modern physics and from Eastern traditions, modern autobiographers have experimented with the possibilities of narrative form as a means of restructuring consciousness through repatterning, and with the ideas of dynamic and organic form as ways of accomodating the constant fact of change.

In this book seven post-World War I autobiographies are presented as examples of crisis narratives which were all regarded by the authors as acts of healing: Vera Brittain's Testament of Youth; Elie Wiesel's Night; Christa Wolf's Kindheitsmuster (A Model Childhood); C.S. Lewis's A Grief Observed; Peter Handke's Wunschloses Unglueck (A Sorrow Beyond Dreams); Adrienne Rich's Of Woman Born; and Robert Pirsig's Zen and the Art of Motorcycle Maintenance. These narratives present a range of crisis situations and a variety of literary strategies but all address the central problems of finding words for the inexpressible, form for the chaotic, and a way out of isolation and despair back into human community through writing. Each demonstrates how therapy and art merge in autobiography, and how in this genre in particular, literature acts back upon life.

A HEALING ART

REGENERATION THROUGH AUTOBIOGRAPHY

INTRODUCTION

AUTOBIOGRAPHY IN OUR TIME

What Life Stories are For

Anyone who has spent much time in planes or buses or in depots where strangers fall into conversation knows something of how people love to tell their life stories. Making experience into story fulfills a variety of human needs: our need to affirm that we are like one another, our need to prove that we are unique, our need to give shape and meaning to raw experience, our need to exercise authority in our own lives by becoming authors of our own stories.

How people tell their stories is never a matter of purely literary interest. It is almost impossible to be interested in autobiography, or even in narrative structure and style, without asking some questions that bridge the disciplinary gap between literature and psychology. Understanding the narrative strategies employed in describing one's own life is, after all, one of the basic projects of psychotherapy.

The questions in which this book originated arose for me a few years ago in the course of reading a series of autobiographical accounts of the Holocaust. These haunting stories of the most extreme and unimaginable kinds of experience touched me not only as evidence of the indomitability and resiliency of the human spirit, but also as testimonies to the power and importance of storytelling as a deeply regenerative human activity. Telling their stories had become a matter of necessity to these writers; again and again they reiterated in their various ways the declarations: "This must be told," "I needed to write this," "I couldn't rest until I recorded what happened to me." But if the extremity and uniqueness of their experience generated a need to speak or write about it, it also presented them with a dilemma: the brutalities they had suffered were "unspeakable," "indescribable," "beyond words," "beyond all telling." The impulse to communicate, intimately linked with survival itself, was coupled with deep frustration at the inadequacy of language and the devices of conventional narrative to convey what had happened. Lawrence Langer summed up the problem neatly in *The Literature of the Holocaust* where he described the victims of Auschwitz as "drifting in a realm beyond analogy."[1]

All marginal experiences or crises necessitate a struggle with language. Crisis breaks down our frames of reference, the strategies we have devised for making sense of the world, and even the descriptive vocabularies we rely upon to communicate our individual perceptions to one another and thus achieve some congruence between inner and outer worlds. Healing therefore involves stretching ordinary language to fit the unconventional and extraordinary.

Since the beginning of time we have used stories and myths to organize the world for ourselves by imposing narrative patterns upon experience. One of the signs of crisis in our time is that so many of our shared stories and formative myths have ceased to command belief or inform action, failing to account satisfactorily for life as we know it. Ira Progoff, a Jungian analyst and pioneer in journal therapy, described the problem as loss of a common language:

> One of the reasons that one person cannot tell another the meaning of life is that in modern times there is so little common framework of discourse in which the ultimate questions of existence can be discussed. The traditional context of beliefs has lost its relevance for large segments of the population. One cannot merely appeal to old doctrines, nor even to the symbolic language of the Bible. It is not that the insights of traditional religion are not true; it is simply that their relevance and meaningfulness is not felt strongly enough in the modern situation of life to be psychologically effective.[2]

Multiplication of autobiographies is one manifestation of the alienation that has resulted from philosophical and religious fragmentation. They represent an attempt on the part of individuals to provide for themselves what the culture fails any longer to provide.

Many twentieth-century autobiographies share a certain urgency because of the atmosphere of apocalyptic anxiety in which they have been written. Modern autobiographers, finding conventional forms and models unsuited to the ragged shape of life in the nuclear age, face the task of revising moral and metaphysical frames of reference; as social consensus and institutions falter we are driven inward to find meaning. In the absence of binding cultural rituals it has become an increasingly important means of supplying the patterning necessary to civilized existence. What Thomas Kuhn has posited about the history of science applies equally well to individual histories--that crisis comes when old paradigms fail.[3]

Autobiography is one available means of restructuring, redescribing, reevaluating, and remythologizing the world. Whereas in traditional societies shared myths and rituals provide meaning by revealing patterns in human experience as paradigms for individual lives, in an alienated culture such as ours autobiography begins to assume this function. In his study of autobiography in America, Thomas Couser calls those autobiographies that serve this function "prophetic." Prophetic autobiography, he claims, flourishes in times of crisis, "when change threatens communal values or when historical developments demand new modes of interpretation. It requires of the autobiographer a sense of his implication in the crisis and a theology or metaphysics capable of comprehending it."[4] Viewed in this way, autobiography appears to be a two-edged tool: it serves to differentiate and validate individual experience against the backdrop of the whole culture, and at the same time to provide new possibilities or precedents by deriving general world views from personal experience. Each of the autobiographies examined in the latter chapters of this book is prophetic in this sense. Each represents an attempt on the part of the writer not only to heal him or herself by transforming crisis into story, but also to speak on behalf of others who have experienced similar life crises.

Of all forms of writing, autobiography seems most clearly to illustrate the inescapable tension between language and experience. Autobiography in any context is a form fraught with unique tensions. It falls in the grey area between fiction and non-fiction, between history and literature, between the private and the public, making it a very slippery area for readers and critics to venture into with their categories, definitions, and rules of thumb. Nor is it clear what are the autobiographer's obligations to his or her audience. Is it more important to give an accurate report or a good story? To provide an edifying example or a useful precedent? The variety of approaches to and uses of autobiography has made it almost imperative that autobiographers explain their intentions, which indeed they do. Most autobiographies open with an apologia, explaining, justifying, or qualifying their claim upon the public, as if the autobiographical act were by definition a kind of presumption needing excuse.

These reflections upon autobiography, and specifically upon crisis narratives, eventually distilled themselves into a series of questions that form the basis of this study: (1) Why does crisis so consistently impel people to write or narrate their stories? (2) What problems does the writer confront in attempting to describe extraordinary experience in ordinary language? (3) What problems or tensions--either psychological or literary--does the autobiographical act itself generate? (4) What is the relationship between the therapeutic and the artistic impulses in stories of crisis? and finally (5) How does the act of writing autobiography contribute to healing? For clearly autobiography can be a healing art--a refuge and a resource for men and women seeking a way to wholeness and stability in periods of confusion, and a way of exercising a very real power over their own destinies.

The Problems of Form

A survey of critical writing about autobiography within the past thirty years reveals that critics and theorists tend to approach it with criteria and rhetoric that differ significantly from those used in the criticism of other literary genres. Most of them agree that the conditions and intentions that produce autobiography distinguish it from other kinds of literary enterprises and that it must therefore be submitted to different standards of judgment.

When Georges Gusdorf wrote his ground-breaking essay, "*Conditions et limites de l'autobiographie* " in 1956, attempting to "sort out the implicit presuppositions of autobiography," he succeeded in defining a number of the questions that have become central in subsequent criticism of autobiography.[5] Those questions covered a variety of approaches to autobiographical texts, considering them in terms of content, context, form, motive, and process. Gusdorf viewed autobiography as a product of certain requisite social and psychological conditions--different from any other literary genre partly because it is so difficult to define, subject to special criteria of judgment because of its unique claims, and linked to life in a way that makes it difficult to discuss it with the same scholarly detachment one might bring to other literary texts. "Style," he writes, "should be understood . . . not only as a principle of writing but as a line of life, a 'life style.'"[6] He progresses from questions of content and context to questions of form and motive, and finally to considering autobiography as a self-reflexive process which "turns back on the life and affects it by a kind of boomerang."[7]

The general direction Gusdorf took in this essay--away from a historical and formal, toward a psychological and process-oriented approach--has been replicated in subsequent criticism of autobiography. Roy Pascal's *Design and Truth in Autobiography* (1960) addresses the question of how the imposition of literary forms and fictionalizing devices obscures or prevents "true" autobiography from being written. But critics were quick to question the terms in which Pascal's questions were posed. Valuable in its own right for its articulation of some of the problems of form in this slippery genre, Pascal's work has often served as a foil for critics who have initiated their own observations by asserting the impossibility of "true" autobiography and the radical relativity of the autobiographical perspective.

While both Gusdorf and Pascal necessarily recognized personal motive as a defining factor in the formation and judgment of autobiography, James Olney's emphasis on this subjective aspect of the autobiographical process brought a fresh, less formally literary slant to the study of autobiography. In his *Metaphors of Self* (1972) and his later anthology, *Autobiography: Essays Theoretical and Critical* (1980) he brought together many of the best autobiography studies undertaken since Gusdorf. Olney's own essay in that collection, "Autobiography and the Cultural Moment," is methodologically eclectic and adopts an interdisciplinary, comparative approach. In it he accomplishes an almost complete shift of emphasis from form to process.

In 1976 Elizabeth Bruss's *Autobiographical Acts: The Changing Situation of a Literary Genre* integrated a study of autobiography as process with a literary historical study of its evolution. In this examination of four autobiographers she spans the history of autobiography since the eighteenth century and traces a trajectory in its evolution by identifying the changing expectations both writers and readers brought to it. Each age, Bruss claims, has produced autobiographies of a particular kind, modifying the genre to meet changing cultural expectations, giving it a different status in the literary canon, and hence producing different kinds and degrees of critical response ranging from virtual dismissal to the acute attention it is now receiving. Ending with Nabokov, Bruss shows how far the genre has progressed in the direction of self-reflexivity and valorization of private rather than public ends. Always a two-directional act, autobiography has never been more self-consciously used and acknowledged as an act performed for the writer as much as for the reader.

Surveys of the development of autobiography, some of which began as far back as St. Augustine, largely left open the question of how or whether twentieth-century autobiographies differ significantly from those written earlier. How have the radical changes in thought and life patterns since World War I changed the way people tell their stories? The autobiographies I have chosen to examine, spanning the decades from World War I to the mid-1970's, share at least three common features that distinguish them from any written previously. First, they demonstrate a degree and kind of self-consciousness only possible in an "age of irony"--a time of radical doubt that subjects all conventions to question. This doubt extends to the most basic assumptions about language and reality, and about the nature of the self. Since post-Freudian psychology has provided a vocabulary for describing the life of the mind in new terms, it has scarcely been possible to write autobiography without reference to those terms and without carefully qualifying any assumption of shared perceptions. Such insistent self-awareness forces the autobiographer to relativize his perspective; it is more difficult than ever to derive dogma from experience, and yet when dogmas prove inadequate it seems to be a persistent human tendency to regenerate them, starting anew with the raw data of personal experience. Therefore, though modern autobiographers may be operating out of less stable frames of reference than their predecessors, they are equally philosophically committed. Indeed, the increasing global anxieties of modern life have given many of them a strong sense of urgency and mission that results in heightened didacticism. But the example they set their readers lies in the act of self-examination itself more than in the conclusions they draw. "The examined life" has become the primary imperative.

A second shared characteristic of modern autobiographies is their frequent focus upon a single critical period rather than upon the entire span of years from childhood onward. In a sense, every autobiography is a story of crisis, in that it recounts change, turning points, conversions, critical lettings-go and breaks with the past; one of the most prominent traditional forms of autobiography is the conversion narrative--an archetypal crisis story. But modern stories of crisis tend to be less teleological, certainly less theological and on the whole less inclined to affix definite meaning to the experience. Because of this narrowed focus, modern autobiographies are often only loosely chronological. Time itself is relativized; past, present and future merge in autobiographical consciousness and the moment of remembering overshadows the moments remembered. Autobiographical strategies have become more candid as autobiographers resort to "metafictional" devices to resolve the ironic discrepancies between form and experience.

This self-conscious focus on process may be a function of a third distinguishing characteristic of modern autobiography, namely that a remarkable number of them have been written toward the beginning rather than at the end of a career. Rather than summary statements or retrospectives, these early works are explorations of possibility. Autobiographies written early and focused upon a single critical period can be a way of seeking and finding self-definition, form, questions, and themes that often go on to be developed further in later work. It is not uncommon for an author to look back upon an early autobiographical work as a groundbreaking effort and to find, as Wiesel did, that the autobiography was the foundation and all the rest "commentary."

In the first chapters of this book three general questions about autobiographical method and the healing potential of autobiography have been addressed. I have tried to explain why autobiography has not only proliferated, but has begun to receive intense critical attention within the past few decades, to explain in what ways autobiography is unique as a literary form, and to suggest some specific ways in which autobiograpical writing can be and has been a healing art.

Seven Exemplary Tales

The seven autobiographical texts used in this study were chosen as representative examples from among a vast body of autobiographical literature written since 1918. They are meant to serve as case studies of the theoretical problems raised. These seven works span a historical period from the 1920's to the 1970's; they include all three basic autobiographical modes: journal, autobiography proper, and autobiographical poetry or fiction--and gradations in between. They are all what I have chosen to call "crisis narratives"--stories focused upon periods of crisis. My explorations of these texts are not evaluative readings so much as efforts to identify the specific tensions and problems common to them in order to understand something essential about the autobiographical act: how it works back upon the writer to regenerate and to heal.

I chose these works with five criteria in mind: I wanted texts that offered clear examples of (l) the healilng dimension of autobiography, (2) different kinds of crises; (3) formal and rhetorical experimentation related to the life processes narrated; (4) the relationship between individual and communal aspects of writing; and (5) literary excellence.

Crisis is the common denominator of the works selected. All the writers had undergone experiences of profound angst, life-threatening danger, grievous loss, despair or mental breakdown, and had recovered to tell their stories. I read each text with a series of questions in mind: Out of what historical, cultural and biographical context was the narrative written? What models of the self are assumed? What literary conventions is the writer employing or subverting? How is extraordinary experience rendered in ordinary language--and what rhetorical problems are raised in the process? How do syntax, structure and imagery reinforce the vision of experience presented? How does silence work as a counterpoint to language--the untold to the told? What are the governing metaphors for crisis and for writing? What does the text reveal about the process of writing? How does the narrative reflect a healing process? How are therapeutic and artistic concerns expressed and balanced? What are the central questions the text poses and answers?

The earliest of the seven is Vera Brittain's *Testament of Youth* (1923), an account of the author's early life and experiences as a combat nurse in World War I. In the course of that war Brittain not only suffered from personal exposure to the extremities of suffering, death, and deprivation in combat areas, she also lost her fiance, her brother, and her best friend--all killed in action. The events chronicled in *Testament* are personal and cultural crises that changed both international politics and the categories that described civilized life. So many hopes were dashed, so much faith lost, and so many lives destroyed, that the terms used to justify, ennoble, or explain such disaster proved woefully inadequate and even ridiçulous. The chivalric ideal, still very much alive in Edwardian

England, began to appear artificial and pretentious, its overwrought concept of honor an incitement to pointless self-destruction. The kind of idealism it fostered led Brittain's fiance, Roland, to claim that "he could wish for no better end than to be found dead in a trench at dawn."[8] Brittain relates this kind of idealistic thinking to "the public school tradition, which stood for militaristic heroism unimpaired by the damping exercise of reason"(99-100).

A new, more dispassionate way of thinking seemed imperative. Hence Brittain's attempt to write a revisionist history that reshapes traditional forms of thought and questions common "truths" by examining the language in which those truths are expressed. She offers, by way of autobiography, a new "reading" of World War I. It is quite literally a reading, for that war was, more than any other, inscribed and rendered in literature written by those directly involved. Such a widely dispersed, amorphous, and chaotic set of events was comprehensible, even to participants, only through the words that gave it shape. The war was inseparable from the stories it generated. Many of those stories took the form of autobiographies, undertaken as attempts to restore some sense of wholeness in a fragmented world.

Written ten years after the armistice and based on both memories and the records she kept in her war diaries, Brittain's book is a legacy to the post-war generation, and an effort to bring to closure and fruition memories whose pain seemed only capable of relief through some kind of transformation--or, as Brittain put it, through being "made useful." Brittain wanted her readers to understand war not as an idea, or a political game, but as the most intense kind of personal suffering multiplied a millionfold.

The narrative falls into three parts, preceded by a fairy tale that serves as an epigraph--the story of "poor Catherine," a young woman given a choice between a happy youth and miserable old age, or an unhappy youth and happy old age. She chooses the latter, reasoning, "If I say a happy youth, then I shall have to suffer the rest of my life. No, I will bear trouble now, and have something better to look forward to." So she gives her decision to the Lady Destiny: "Give me a happy old age." Against this parabolic backdrop, Brittain proceeds to tell her own story of unhappy youth from the perspective of a survivor. She is committed to living out the second chance life has given her, according to insights gained through the crises of the war years. Her methods and sensibilities are typically modernist--ironic, eclectic, disillusioned, but for all that ultimately idealistic. The book is a retrospective by a woman still young whose youth seems a lifetime away.

Another woman's account of war experience, comparable in intent and intensity to Brittain's is Christa Wolf's *A Model Childhood* (1980) (*Kindheitsmuster*, 1979). In this daring, experimental narrative the writer explores her early years in East Prussia under Hitler's expanding power. She confronts a past that has laden her with guilt and attempts to reestablish connection with a part of herself she has long rejected. In the text she divides her self into three personae: the first person who narrates, the second person, to whom the narrative is addressed, and the third person, herself as a child, who is the subject of the narrative. At the end of the book Wolf reflects upon her attempt to reclaim her past through writing:

> The child who was hidden in me--has she come forth? Or has she been scared into looking for a deeper, more inaccessible hiding place? . . . And the past, which can still split the first person into the second and the third--has its hegemony been broken? Will the voices be still?9

Like Brittain, Wolf also attempts to link the past to the future. She takes her daughter, Lenka, with her on a journey back in time and space to the scenes of her childhood. Lenka thus serves as audience and foil in Wolf's process of self-discovery and self-disclosure. The critic Peter Graves wrote of *A Model Childhood* ,

> It is a reckoning with a past that still haunts and, with the presence of Lenka, an attempt to explain to a

> contemporary teenager how these things could have happened. The confrontation of two epochs in the form of mother and daughter is one of the book's greatest strengths.

Graves calls it "a courageous book that breaks taboos and ... is infused with an integrity and a deep moral concern that raise it far above the narrow and self-conscious partisanship of much of GDR literature."[10]

Elie Wiesel's *Night* (1955) is a third war story that becomes a reflection upon memory, responsibility, and suffering, and an effort, through re-creation, to heal the shattered self. The narrative is composed of a series of discrete vignettes that allow the reader glimpses of the writer's descent into hell from his childhood in the Hungarian town of Sighet, through ghettoization, deportment, camp "selections," the manifold brutalities of camp life, the death of his father, his loss of faith, and finally the ambiguous relief of liberation in 1945. The small book is an experiment in distillation and, by means of its calculated silences and omissions, a reminder of how far the evil imagination of man exceeds the limitations of language.[11]

In 1945 Wiesel vowed to wait at least ten years before attempting to write about what he had witnessed at Auschwitz. He believed that no one as close as he was then to the experience could convey the truth about it without diminishment or falsification.[12] Later, however, he came to regard the task of remembering and writing about those months of humiliation and imprisonment as a vocation. Wiesel summed up the paradox that underlies his work by telling one interviewer, "You must speak, but how can you when the full story is beyond language?" He went on to explain his sense of vocation in this way: "We survivors believe that if we survived, we must do something with our lives. The first task is to tell the tale."[13]

C.S. Lewis's *A Grief Observed* (1980) and Peter Handke's *A Sorrow Beyond Dreams* (1974) (*Wunschloses Unglueck*, 1972) are survival tales of a different kind. Both were written in the wake of great personal loss:

Lewis's after his new wife's death of bone cancer, and Handke's after his mother's suicide. In form, style, and ideology the two texts differ markedly, but they address similar concerns. To both writers grief is not only a burden but a challenge to be met; it poses moral, intellectual, and eventually artistic problems. Both explain that they have turned to writing as a means of clarifying those problems and working out solutions. Since both men are writers, writing is the obvious way for them to accomplish their "grief work"--a term Freud originated to describe the necessary and inevitable stages of regaining emotional equilibrium after bereavement. The processes of composition, description, narration, and argument are familiar tasks. Through the performance of these tasks they regain some measure of control over powerful, chaotic feelings.[14,15]

Both texts reflect the divided consciousness that results from the self-alienation grief often generates. As death divides one life from another, so bereavement can also divide the emotional side of the self, which feels the loss, from the intellect, which attempts to adjust to death by accounting for it. The self who acts--the writer--is separated from the self who suffers. One of these selves questions; the other answers. In Lewis's journal, the doubter is in dialogue with the believer; in Handke's, a son who asks why his mother took her life is in dialogue with an empathetic biographer who reconstructs her life in order to provide the answer. Each text thus has a double objective: Lewis's is both a quarrel with God and an apologia; Handke's is both a story about his mother's life and a story about his own. The overarching task the writers set themselves is to bring the two sides of the divided self back into congruence and thereby regain some measure of peace.

Robert Pirsig's *Zen and the Art of Motorcycle Maintenance* (1974) shares with Lewis's and Handke's works this objective of reunifying a divided self, though it is very different from either of them in structure and tone. The book's subtitle, "An Inquiry into Values," suggests its hybrid character: its grander, more general aim is to articulate a comprehensive phenomenology capable of bridging the great divisions between Eastern and Western modes of thought and between what Pirsig calls "classical" and "romantic" visions of reality. Its expressed secondary aim is to heal the writer's breach with his own past and to reconnect him with the self he lost through mental breakdown, institutionalization, and shock therapy. Like Christa Wolf, Pirsig gives his former self a name and speaks of that self in the third person. Paradoxically, his objectification of "Phaedrus," that other self, works, as does Wolf's split image of her self, as a step toward reintegration of personality. Pirsig's long, meandering narrative, in which the description of a cross-country motorcycle trip is contrapuntally interspersed with lengthy philosophical reflections, traces the dialectical process of recovering and articulating a vision of reality that Phaedrus saw but could not find a way to communicate. Therein it also becomes an effort to neutralize and reclaim an excised portion of the writer's personal past.[16]

Like *A Model Childhood*, *Zen* also links past with future, fashioning a personal vision and personal history into a legacy for the next generation. Pirsig takes his son, Chris, along on his journey. He is separated from Chris, as from Phaedrus, by communication barriers he seeks to overcome in the course of the journey. Chris anchors him in present, external reality while Phaedrus pulls him inward and backward in time. Between these two forces the writer seeks a balance point where the vision he lost can be recovered and communicated without his losing himself in its vast network of cosmic implications.

George Steiner called *Zen* "the legend of a great hunt after identity, after the salvation of mind and soul out of obsession, the hunter being hunted; a fiction repeatedly interrupted by, enmeshed with, a lengthy meditation on the ironic and tragic singularities of American man . . ."[17] That characterization makes clear the dialectical quality of autobiographical writing, manifested not only in the persistent doubleness of theme, voice, and narrative stance, but also in the entwining of two distinct modes of discourse.

Personal and historical past are similarly intertwined in Adrienne Rich's *Of Woman Born* (1977) where a chapter in the author's life story assumes mythic dimensions for her, and becomes the basis of a systematic philosophy. The book's subtitle, "Motherhood as Experience and Institution," adumbrates the kind of intertwining she accomplishes in this autobiography-as-cultural history. In its autobiographical aspect the narrative is a journey back into the early years of marriage and motherhood when the young poet began to experience deep conflicts between her inner life and the imprisoning expectations and definitions imposed upon her by assigned social and familial roles. Driven to the edge of insanity and violence by the deep frustrations those conflicts engendered, she took refuge in her journal. The more mature writer reads and reflects upon those journals with profound sympathy for the person she once was, retrospectively attempting to heal the wounds those years inflicted. She is able now to take a wider view of her own suffering. She speaks passionately, but with the relative detachment time has granted, about the plight of all women as represented in her own story. The book is thus an elaboration and an examination of the outcries that resound in the poetry and journal entries of those difficult years--an attempt, among other things, to heal bitterness by turning suffering into a testament.[18]

Diverse as they are, some significant common denominators unify these "crisis narratives" which, examined as such, may illuminate something about what I would call the "poetics" of crisis. Each is a working out or a working through of an experience that fundamentally changed the writer. Each of the writers regards his or her personal crisis as a significant example of the human situation, and hence as representative, useful, and worthy of public attention. All the works are highly self-conscious and unabashedly self-reflexive; the writers discuss writing as they write, focusing on the process of writing as a means of achieving wholeness or healing. All are therefore directly concerned with paradoxes and problems of definition, linguistic and literary forms and conventions, the implications of various modes of discourse, the powers and insufficiencies of language and uses of silence, and the sacramental efficacy of image, metaphor, and symbol. All of them seek to move beyond conventional discourse and received categories, particularly their own habitual categories of thought. All are examining basic assumptions they once held and how those assumptions changed, working against the cultural and personal myths that have entrapped them, and, by getting outside those myths, opening doors to new ways of structuring consciousness. They seek to invent a mode of description that is holistic and open-ended--one that separates description from judgment and challenges conventional categories. They strive for a "middle voice," between the active and the passive, expressive of the individual's ontological situation, poised between fate and freedom--a voice capable of expressing something happening in which the subject is both participant and object--that expresses, as Gertrude Stein put it, "being becoming." They train their mental vision in multiple directions, interweaving different levels of consciousness in an attempt to express the unboundedness and instability of any given version of reality. Writing thus becomes for them a way of seeing, demonstrating the survival value of "negative capability"--the ability to perceive, acknowledge, and communicate paradox, ambiguity, and contradiction without, as Keats put it, "straining after certainties."

My hypothesis as I began this project and my conviction after many rereadings of these texts, is that crisis tends to generate experimental modes of thinking and writing because it breaks down philosophical and linguistic categories, shatters assumptions, and disorganizes the inner world. The two most obvious responses to such breakdown would be either to reassert the old paradigms or to try to construct new ones more comprehensive and more flexible than the old. If this century has produced any fundamental changes in values, they have gone in the direction of accepting and valuing flexibility, uncertainty, and paradox over stabilizing dogma.

Some of the most influential philosophical paradigms of our time are analogous to those in new physics which has revealed that two mutually exclusive states can coexist (as in the wave/particle paradox)--that our neat schematics falsify reality, and that totally objective measurement is impossible. Our descriptive categories themselves create blind spots. The "uncertainty principle" which implies the inescapability of subjectivity and hence distortion, has become a powerful metaphor in every area of serious thought from theology and metaphysics to medicine and politics, and has penetrated to the very roots of the literary enterprise where the nature of statement is always under scrutiny. The consequent relativism has been reiterated in virtually every field of inquiry. In art and literature the result has been what some would describe as a kind of ironic neoromanticism, a revalorization of the individual perspective. Such a stance is deeply threatening to our oldest cultural institutions and traditional modes of thought.

The traditional thinking sacralized by our most powerful institutions has to do with grasping a vision and fixing it--reinforcing it against change, holding and preserving, extending it in time. The importance of continuity and stability are assumed; hence institutions tend by their nature to resist change. People who have been through radical change can no longer comfortably define themselves in terms of the stabilities institutions offer. To live with change they need to find a way of thinking about it that allows them both to recognize the extent of its implications and also to retain the continuity necessary to an intact sense of identity. The task of restructuring consciousness places enormous demands on a person's spiritual vitality. The seven writers whose works form the core of this study are all people who sought to meet those demands through the mediation of autobiography--a form in constant flux, relativistic by definition, and perhaps, therefore, a particularly representative and appropriate form of writing for our time.

The Form of the Problem

The texts chosen fell so naturally into chronological sequence that the obvious procedure seemed at first to be to examine them in terms of historical context, each autobiography clearly being the product not only of a personal, but also of a cultural crisis. However the relative simplicity of historical chronology as an organizing principle was deceptive. Although the cultural phenomena I adopted as points of reference did provide a useful framework within which to interpret modern autobiography and its therapeutic uses, historical classification would have led into a sociology of autobiography rather than into a more general theory of the relationship between the dynamics of crisis and literary strategies. In order to clarify that relationship, I needed to focus not upon the different circumstances of the crises the writers were describing, but upon what those circumstances and those descriptions had in common.

Two questions rose to the top of the heap: What do all crisis experiences have in common, and what do the dynamics of crisis have to do with the design of narrative? To answer these questions I tried first to reconstruct inferentially the "stages" of crisis as described by each writer, trying to determine whether indeed there were identifiable stages common to the experiences I grouped under that name. Reading through the various descriptions of crises, I found that they were all predicated upon one of two alternative archetypes or models. The first of these was the notion of crisis as descent and reascent. This more traditional model derives directly from the mythic archetype of descent into the underworld. Perceived in this way the experience of crisis appears to occur in three stages: (1) descent: a stage of loss, degeneration, and increasing confusion; (2) stasis: a period of spiritual paralysis, isolation, and silence; (3) reascent: an experience of epiphany or paradigmatic shift, a new gestalt of problem and solution, radical redefinition of assumptions, and spiritual regeneration resulting in the ability to relate to the world in a new and more comprehensive way. This orderly notion of crisis is certainly aesthetically satisfying, implying as it does a rather neat sequence of events that moves steadily toward resolution and closure. However it overschematizes, as mythic patterns tend to, a complex, and even chaotic, process.

An alternative model of crisis, more common in modern writing and more aligned with the principles of literary modernism, is implied in Vera Brittain's description of the war experience as "the smashing up of my youth," or in Eliot's description of the post-war world as "a heap of broken images," or in Yeats's characterization of the intellectual and spiritual anarchy in the modern world: "Things fall apart; / The centre cannot hold." These metaphors suggest a more extreme vision of crisis, one that lacks the ordered teleological implications of the mythic descent and reascent. But the stages in the experience are similar. After things "fall apart," one is left isolated and adrift in a metaphysical void. To survive one needs to construct some new vision of reality as a basis on which to begin to reassemble the fragments of his shattered world into a new design.

Both models of crisis suggest a metamorphic progression involving decomposition and recomposition, or dismemberment and re-membering. It is not hard to see how autobiography might serve as a means of accomplishing that recomposition since it begins in the act of remembering. It can also be a form of purgation--a healing and purifying act by which the contents of personal history and belief are filtered through a new set of terms, and irrelevancies--old guilts and old inhibitions, left aside. It can in fact be an act of transformation, literally making new forms like new wineskins to hold a new wine that would sour in the old. The next question, therefore, was how the various forms these autobiographies took reflected the several phases of periods of crisis, and how, if at all, these forms might be a function of the different stages at which writers took up their pens. It seems fairly clear that at least in broad terms, the three basic autobiographical forms--journal, autobiography proper, and autobiographical fiction or poetry--correspond to three different stages in the healing or transformative process. They are, respectively, the results of three distinct modes of thought: introspection, retrospection, and transformation. In each mode a different kind of literary act is performed and a different stage in healing enacted. Viewed as a sequence, these modes of thought and writing successively indicate greater authorial control and more aesthetic distance from the image of the self presented in the text.

As two of the authors studied here explicitly attest, journals or diaries are often survival tools. Vera Brittain claims that her diary virtually kept her alive in periods of extreme frustration, and Peter Handke writes that he embarked upon a journal in the midst of his grief "because having something to do brings me back to life." Journals tend to be more self-reflexive, less patterned or artful than other forms of autobiography.

Accounts of crises that appear in the pages of journals are written from "within" the event, at a time when the writer is immersed, sometimes nearly overwhelmed, by the experiences he attempts to record. C.S. Lewis, for instance, wrote out his grief day by day, one thought at a time, in disconnected or very loosely connected paragraphs as need dictated because, as he said, "By writing it all down I believe I get a little outside it." Such journal entries are generally a first and rough attempt to give experience syntax and shape, to externalize it in an effort to regain perspective and control.

Writing in a diary often focuses primarily on the "what" of the event recorded--the facts. Simple description precedes other acts of composition. The objective is to "get it down" or "get it out." The writing of a diarist is thus both exploratory and purgative. It is a means of seeing, an act of naming, and an effort to sketch boundaries around an event by giving it narrative form. The aim and effect of such writing is often relief and reassurance since writing can familiarize an extraordinary experience by subjecting it to conventionalizing categories and to analogies.

Autobiographies proper differ in some obvious ways from journals: they are written not from "within" the event, but from a vantage point where the writer can look back and see its contours. He or she can thus give the experience a beginning, middle, and end, and so take on the persona of "objective" narrator. The autobiographer is generally focused more than the diarist on the "how" than the "what" of the experience; formal and literary concerns are more prominent. Exploration gives way to review and analysis. Writers' own descriptions of the autobiographical process frequently include words that emphasize repetition and transformation: remembering, reconstructing, revising. The focus on how things happened leads the writer into problems of form and structure, and forces him or her to clarify an organizing principle in order to achieve narrative coherence. The autobiographer's objective is generally more complicated; the aims of autobiography proper include more than simple survival. For whatever the imagined audience, the journal is a private form, and autobiography public. In the former, expression itself is primary, whereas in the latter communication, comprehensibility, coherence, and effectiveness contribute to shaping the story.

As the writer's concerns widen to include matters of form, style, and syntax, spiritual and psychological problems are translated into literary problems; cosmic issues become concrete and present themselves as a series of stylistic choices. This is usually more true as the writer gains distance from the event he or she describes. "Distance" here means the ability to reshape and control the raw data of experience to meet specifically artistic criteria. The ability to attend to formal questions is not, of course, simply an index of how much aesthetic distance has been gained; it can also be a means of gaining distance from that which threatens to overwhelm.

The metamorphosis from victimization to authorship is successful when the artistic motives overtake the therapeutic. Fictionalization requires considerable aesthetic distance. This is not to say that fiction is necessarily a more sophisticated, comprehensive, or objective form, only that, when one considers fiction-making as a stage in recovery of one's perspective, voice, and authority, it seems to represent a more complicated act of externalizing and objectifying experience. Wiesel, for instance, wrote five novels based upon his experience of the Holocaust after the publication of *Night*, and though they lack nothing in passionate intensity, the later ones are increasingly fictionalized, increasingly removed from the data of his personal history. To fictionalize his own life a writer needs, in some sense, to have "let go" of it. In fiction memory gives way to imagination, what was to what might be, factuality to possibility. When he is able to transform his personal crisis into a work of art the writer has taken possession of the thing that threatened to possess him. In the text he has defined another world, become a creator, an agent, an originator. When he has done that, the purgative ritual is complete; the danger is consigned to story, and some measure of healing, one assumes, is accomplished--if it is true, as Isak Dinessen said, that "all sorrows can be borne when they are put into a story."

Though the stages of recovery seem to bear significant correspondence to the various forms of autobiography, using these stages to categorize autobiographies can result in too schematic a view of both the autobiographical act and the process of healing. All the autobiographers studied here were, after all, struggling with complex and chaotic feelings. Their processes and methods were not as neat as these categorizations might suggest. While there may be distinct stages in healing, the process is also many-layered and kaleidescopically shifting. In attempting to answer my own original question--how writers may use autobiography as a healing agent, I found myself involved, like them, in a search for appropriate models and metaphors. So I turned the critical kaleidescope once again and took yet another view of the autobiographical act: I began to think of it in terms of its various "layers" rather than its stages. This led me to my final organizing principle, which was to examine the autobiographical process in terms of the multiple problems and decisions that the autobiographer confronts simultaneously in his or her effort to write whole; in other words, to think of the autobiographical act in terms of density rather than development.

How Autobiographies Happen

I revised my original questions: What is involved in writing a life story? What kinds of literary problems have to be confronted? What is the spectrum of concerns that emerge and converge in the autobiographical process? Every writer must concern him- or herself with composition, language, theme, structure, and certainly with his own motives or aims. But how are these concerns peculiarly operative in autobiography--specifically in accounts of crisis?

I began with the role of memory and imagination. Remembering and imagining are acts of composition: out of the ragbag of memory images and incidents are selected, arranged, and begin to be woven into a whole fabric. For the writer as artist, composition is fiction-making. For the writer as a person, it is, at its most authentic, a process of discovering a layer of his or her own truth, his or her own history, that he or she unearths like an archaeologist and begins to interpret. The remembered past becomes raw material for a personal mythology in the making.

Screening memories and struggling with language are efforts to answer questions that are, for a time, the motivating forces in these writers' lives. Every book is an answer to a question; for the author, arriving at the right question is often a long process of exploration. Wiesel compares himself to Job, a man whose wisdom consisted of questioning. Questions, he insists, are far more important than answers. In every autobiography lie the thematic questions that give a life its shape. Christa Wolf asks, "How did we become what we are?" Handke asks, reviewing his mother's life, What are the roots of despair? How do we get beneath the surfaces of one another's lives? Adrienne Rich asks, What are the myths that entrap us and prevent our recognizing our own realities--and how do we get outside them? Identifying the constellating questions in each of these works made me increasingly aware of autobiography as a quest--not only for answers, but for questions that allow new ways of seeing and describing experience.

Narrating a life story can thus be seen as an essentially dialectical process. A narrative moves by implicitly posing and answering questions. The shape of the narrative is itself a part of the answer as it gives new form to experience and thereby reveals new dimensions of it. Particularly for modern autobiographers, for whom "post-historical" self-consciousness and "post-Christian" metaphysical uncertainty make it impossible to assume even the most basic narrative patterns as ontological givens, structure itself is inevitably a form of statement. Handke's narrative, for instance, with its five-part concentric structure, is about penetration to a center--and about emptiness at the center--about surfaces and interiors. Pirsig's "inquiry into values" likewise has an expressive structure: the narration oscillates between the inner and the outer life, between the journey onward and the journey inward.

Connection between the inner and the outer life, individual and community, is another object of the autobiographical act. An autobiography is, in Emily Dickinson's phrase, a "letter to the world." Particularly when crisis has isolated an individual within the confines of his or her own nearly incommunicable situation, autobiography reestablishes relationship with a sustaining community and leads the author out of self-imprisonment back into a larger context. Self and public are both audiences for the autobiographer; being alone and being connected are the two poles of experience and the text becomes a bridge between the two.

---

1 Lawrence Langer, *The Holocaust and the Literary Imagination* (New Haven: Yale University Press, 1975), p. 7.

2 Ira Progoff, *The Symbolic and the Real* (New York: Julian Press, Inc., 1963), p. 14.

3 Thomas Kuhn, *The Structure of Scientific Revolutions* (Chicago: University of Chicago Press, 1962).

4 Thomas Couser, *American Autobiography: The Prophetic Mode* (Amherst: University of Massachusetts Press, 1979), p. 3.

5 Georges Gusdorf, "Conditions and Limits of Autobiography," in James Olney, ed., *Autobiography: Essays Theoretical and Critical* (Princeton: Princeton University Press, 1980), p. 28.

6 Gusdorf, p. 47.

7 Gusdorf, p. 47.

8 Vera Brittain, *Testament of Youth* (London: Virago, Ltd., 1978), p. 117. All further references to this work will be found in the text.

9 Christa Wolf, *A Model Childhood* , trans. Ursule Molinaro and Hedwig Rappolt (New York: Farrar, Strauss and Giroux, 1980), p. 406. All further references to this work will be found in the text.

10 Peter Graves, cited in *Contemporary Authors* , vol. 85-88, ed. Frances C. Locher (Detroit: Glae Research Co., 1980), p. 87.

[11] Eliue Wiesel, *Night* , trans. Stella Rodway (New York: Bantam Books, 1960). All further references to this work will be found in the text.

[12] Elie Wiesel, in an interview with Harry James Cargas, *Harry James Cargas in Conversation with Elie Wiesel* (New York: Paulist Press, 1976), pp. 87-88.

[13] Elie Wiesel, cited in *Contemporary Authors* , vol. 7-8, Revised Series, ed. Evory and Metzger (Detroit: Gale Research Co., 1980).

[14] C.S. Lewis, *A Grief Observed* (New York: Bantam Books, 1980), p. 10. All further references to this work will be found in the text.

[15] Peter Handke, *A Sorrow Beyond Dreams* , trans. Ralph Manheim (New York: Farrar, Strauss and Giroux, 1974), p. 5. All further references to this work will be found in the text.

[16] Robert Pirsig, *Zen and the Art of Motorcycle Maintenance: An Inquiry into Values* (New York: Bantam Books, 1974). All further references to this work will be found in the text.

[17] George Steiner, cited in *Contemporary Authors*, vol. 53-56, ed. Clare D. Kinsman (Detroit: Gale Research Co., 1975), p. 466.

[18] Adrienne Rich, *Of Woman Born: Motherhood as Experience and Institution* (New York: Bantam Books, 1976). All further references to this work will be found in the text.

CHAPTER 1

WRITING TO HEAL

Operative Metaphors

In the introduction to his autobiographical work, *Montauk* , Max Frisch writes that the work was "a kind of therapy accompanying the acceptance of my own life."[1] Frisch's explanation of his autobiographical impulse is typical of an overwhelming number of modern autobiographers who embark upon their life stories as a form of self-therapy. Vera Brittain, for instance, described her now famous wartime diary as a refuge--indeed, a survival tool--during the worst days of the war: "the only remaining resource was my . . . diary. I . . . poured into it the chaotic wretchedness which had, as so often before, no other outlet" (340).

The therapeutic value of autobiographical writing is made quite explicit by many writers who regard that purpose as a justification of their enterprise. Anais Nin attributes her whole writing career to a therapeutic initiative, calling her writing a "necessary part of living," a habit acquired during a sickly adolescence when writing became "a way of learning to live."[2]

As Nin traced the therapeutic core of her autobiographical impulse to the beginning of her career, so Carl Jung discovered anew the healing properties of writing in the autobiography he began in old age--a work which he at first resisted writing, then reluctantly undertook at the persistent requests of his colleagues, and finally found to be indispensable to his own well-being:

> It has become a necessity for me to write down my early memories. If I neglect to do so for a single day, unpleasant physical symptoms immediately follow. As soon as I set to work they vanish and my head feels perfectly clear. . . . Something within me has been touched. A gradient has formed, and I must write.[3]

Narration has always been an aspect of healing. The ancient Greeks believed that the expressive arts drew healing energy from the gods. Most tribal peoples still believe that, and healing dances and storytelling rituals occupy an important place in their communal life. Kenneth Burke and Langdon Elsbree, among others, have traced a direct line of relationship between modern narration and primitive healing rituals.[4] In Elsbree's study of narrative and ritual autobiography is recognized as one among many modes of healing through storytelling, including "the confession, the apologia, . . . the shaman taming the demons of the collective unconscious, the therapist, local comrade, or evangelist leading the group in self-examination."[5] Autobiography might be regarded as an evolutionary development of these other forms of healing, peculiarly suited to the temper of our times.

Although healing is among the oldest and most universal of human concerns, however, practitioners of healing arts have never universally agreed upon what constitutes health and healing. This lack of consensus attests to the extraordinary complexity of the healing process. The most common diagnostic terms used in medicine and psychotherapy employ a wide range of metaphors for describing illness or disease, each of which implies a slightly different notion of how healing takes place. The terms disease, disorder, or breakdown, for instance, examined etymologically or metaphorically, suggest slightly different conceptions of illness. Moreover, as any diagnostic metaphor implies a particular notion of disease, so it also implies a particular therapeutic approach--one which will complete the metaphor. So, for instance, if we describe a problem as atrophy, the healing act will be to reconstitute; if imbalance, it will be to restore balance; if deficiency, it will be to supplement; if fragmentation, it will be to reintegrate.

Autobiographical strategies, like medical and therapeutic methods, depend upon this same kind of metaphorical equation. As healing gestures autobiographies are doubly metaphoric, for they not only translate the act of healing into literary terms, they also, by virtue of their various narrative strategies, imply particular images of the healing process, i.e. purging, restoring, reviving. As in medicine itself, these diagnostic metaphors are predicated upon a particular conception of the nature of the problem and produce particular strategies for its solution.

Simply analyzing the writing process in terms of the various discrete choices entailed in the act of composition reveals how close the analogy is between writing and healing. Writing can be purgative, restorative, reconstructive, integrative, transformative, and the basic elements of narrative--pattern, design, structure, closure, coherence, balance--all means of making whole.

In the process of composing an autobiography, a writer may move through a variety of modes of writing that signal a progression toward broader perspective and greater control--from exploration to reflection to analysis to speculation. At each stage questions arise: What has happened to me? Why did it happen? How can I relate these events to the rest of my life? How can I communicate my experience to others, and why should it be told? The writer moves from the initial task of finding words and images to patterning them, and finally to forming a gestalt that brings many discrete elements of experience under one rubric to make them a narrative that can be perceived as a single whole with interactive parts.

The three stages of healing most closely replicated in the crisis narratives examined here are catharsis, or purgation; restoration or return to wholeness; and transformation, or making new. These three terms, more exactly than any others, serve to describe the healing action of autobiography, each roughly corresponding to a stage in the process of composition.

Purging

The first, and most obvious step in healing by writing is catharsis--purging or cleansing--one of the oldest and most common methods of curing body and mind. Since ancient times purification has been recognized as a crucial aspect of healing. Autobiography purges by externalizing forces which, held inside, would poison or corrupt: evil memories, fears, fantasies, anxieties. Commenting upon the cathartic function of autobiography, critic Richard Church writes,

> the very process of self-revelation acts . . . as a kind of confessional, whose cathartic effect brings health and new life to the penitent. For indeed autobiography, by the very pain involved in the exploration, is a form of penitence, especially for those who tend to be self-concerned. The purgation has a purifying effect and gives the individual a clarity of mind which augurs well for his future relationships with his fellow creatures.[6]

Relief of guilt is one common form purgation takes. Cultural and literary critic Alfred Kazin claims that guilt, being a peculiarly pervasive affliction among Americans, is causally related to the abundance of confessional literature in our culture: "Guilt seems more endemic than it ever did. It is certainly more popular. Why? No doubt it makes possible a confessional literature that is self-dramatizing in the absence of moral authority."[7] Autobiography, we may infer, is becoming more widespread because it provides a cathartic outlet previously institutionalized in the confessional, and therefore serves a necessary social function. As a more loosely defined and more personalized release from guilt, it corresponds to the needs of an atomized society in which individualism approaches the status of a religion: the penitent retains authority over the form of his penance, expressing in his penitential act both humility and spiritual autonomy. The autobiographer acts as his or her own priest and physician, responding in a literary act to the challenge, "Heal thyself."

Explicitly purgative writing, such as that in journals where the writer is declaredly working through a period of suffering or crisis, often displays only minimal concern for formal balance or structure. The units of thought are brief--often single, unconnected sentences. Beginnings and endings are abrupt. Intense focus on the immediate results in a pre-narrative form, often lacking logical or chronological order. Such texts are frequently self-contradictory. The writing is exploratory: a means of sorting out and naming feelings, seeking to grasp the experience through description. Journals are also frequently obtrusively self-reflexive: the process of writing itself becomes a dominant theme.

Healing through catharsis is, of course, one of the bases of psychoanalysis. Freud's psychoanalytic method, originally known as his "talking cure," was designed to provide outlets for the repressed material that caused sickness. The close and suggestive analogies between psychotherapy and writing are apparent. The process of writing an autobiography is, after all, very similar to what takes place in a therapist's office--the telling of personal history and progressive recognition, articulation, and acknowledgement of meaningful patterns that emerge in the telling.

In both cases the undertaking reveals or produces meaningful structures and patterns of imagery. And in both cases the structuring and patterning not only serve to shape the past, but also affect the present and future life of the teller. Both processes serve not only to enhance understanding, but also to effect change.

Some important distinctions between confessional autobiography and psychotherapy do need to be recognized, however. While both are processes of re-vision, autobiography takes the process a step further in accommodating to the conventions of literary discourse, and artistic composition becomes as important as cathartic expression. Moreover, in autobiography, transference--so essential to the psychoanalytic process as Freud defined it--cannot be reproduced because of the solitary nature of the autobiographical act.[8] The analogy between autobiography and psychotherapy, therefore, needs to be drawn with considerable qualification. Nevertheless, though the basic process of dismembering and remembering that takes place in therapy is also the essential action of autobiography, the two are converging: modern psychiatry is turning again to "expressive arts therapy" as a legitimate area of research.

Recognizing the therapeutic potential of autobiographical writing, a number of psychologists and psychotherapists have attempted to incorporate it into their practice as a systematic form of therapy. One such effort in this country, Ira Progoff's "Intensive Journal" method, is a "writing cure" analogous in many ways to Freud's "talking cure." Progoff claims that the act of writing one's own life story initiates a dynamic dialectical process by means of which the writer can become deeply engaged in a process of healing, self-discovery, and growth. The efficacy of such a practice depends, he claims, upon the kinds of narrative structures involved, the way in which imagery is arrived at and employed, and a certain axiomatic attitude toward writing as an act of exploration, and not necessarily as conclusive statement.

Progoff's own work on journal therapy is an effort to maximize the efficiency with which writing can be employed as an instrument for mental and spiritual health. He makes an interesting distinction between conventional forms and uses of the journal and the highly differentiated form he has developed. Traditionally, he claims, journals have been used as instruments of self-justification or reinforcement of fixed attitudes, limiting rather than enlarging the possibilities of personality and insulating individuals from questions they did not want to face. "The tendency of journals to turn in upon their own subjectivity . . . and move in circular patterns," he writes, "is a common pitfall that must be borne in mind."[9] Progoff claims that his own method, which provides highly articulated structures for generating and enhancing internal dialogue, avoids this pitfall and makes the journal an instrument of growth rather than of self-protection. His caveat here suggests an important qualification to my own thesis: as with other potential means of healing, autobiography can be put to various ends, some of which may ultimately be destructive. It is by no means the case that the act in and of itself heals automatically. Honesty is a complex business, the more so in proportion to the complexity of the medium of expression; simplicity and "whole sight" are only won by steadfast resistance to the pressures of the narrative form to fulfill its own demands for symmetry and completion.

Restructuring

Wholeness, an ancient principle in medicine and a ruling metaphor in psychotherapy, is also a formative notion in the construction of personal narratives. Hemingway's remark that writing personal history is to make experience "come out right," makes the point very simply: that the traditional function of narrative is to endow formless experience with balance and closure by making it into a completed story with beginning, middle, and end. Besides providing aesthetic satisfaction, this translation of life into writing sets the writer outside his or her experience by setting the experience outside the self, granting a certain objectivity and perhaps inuring the writer to some of its pain.

The end of a well-constructed story bears a direct relationship to the beginning: the conclusion completes the equation the exposition implies. This kind of symmetry is no less important in autobiography than in fiction, though it is a fictive device. Any story, however "true," is, as one critic put it, "beholden to certain imperatives of imaginative discourse."[10]

The autobiographer's attempt to construct an artfully shaped, balanced narrative represents, moreover, a secondary stage in healing. The writer is more nearly healed whose focus has begun to shift from the content of the experience to the problems of composition. Shaping a narrative may be assumed to involve a degree of detachment greater than is needed to write a journal. The writer adopts a more active attitude toward his or her material, establishes criteria for inclusion and exclusion of available material, records events in such a way as to reveal certain patterns and tends to suppress those that don't fit those patterns, and by this process often achieves aesthetic distance from his or her own pain. The "patient who suffers" becomes an agent of his or her own healing.

Structuring a narrative is a deliberate and authoritative act. As Jonathan Culler observes, "Structures and relations are not objective properties of external objects; they emerge only in a structuring process."[11] Even in a nonfictional form, this process activates a writer's creative faculties. Olney suggests that an autobiographer "half discovers, half creates a deeper design and truth than adherence to historical and factual truth could ever make claim to . . ."[12] A balanced narrative traces a fine line between artifice and accuracy in order to achieve this truth that is revealed only in and by design.

Desire for balance is one aspect of the general longing for wholeness fundamental to the notion of self implied in most psychologies, medicine, philosophy, and theology. We have, as Janet Varner Gunn puts it, a "compulsion toward wholeness" that expresses itself in literature as in every other human endeavor. The ideal of wholeness, which in this age of fragmentation and inconclusiveness we may have come to regard with some skepticism, has been a central and profound human longing since Plato and Aristotle, and "is part and parcel of all our sense-making activity as human beings."[13]

Among the various schools of psychotherapy, Jungian psychology most vigorously adopts the metaphor of wholeness in explaining the healing process. In *Aion* Jung writes:

> Although "wholeness" seems at first sight to be nothing but an abstract idea. . . , it is nevertheless empirical in so far as it is anticipated by the psyche in the form of spontaneous or autonomous symbols."[14]

Jung calls these symbols of wholeness "mandalas." They appear in myths, religious rites, dreams, stories, and art. They are characterized by quaternity, closure, symmetry, balance, and centripetal movement. Every culture, Jung claims, has public symbols of this nature--from the circular symbol of the Tao to the Christian cross, to the medicine wheels of American Indian tribes. Individuals, too, he observes, spontaneously generate private mandala symbols when they are in need of spiritual healing, "chiefly during times of psychic disorientation or reorientation."[15] A narrative structure can serve the same function--can indeed become a "mandala" by providing to the disparate elements of experience center, pattern, and perimeters.

Symbolizing

If we understand the act of designing a narrative structure as one way of achieving "wholeness" through written expression, there is a complementary way, more organic, by which unity is achieved not so much through structures as through the repetition and resonance of certain centralizing motifs. An experience of wholeness can come about through the generation and recognition of what Jung would call "symbols of transformation" that unify the story of a life by providing imaginative axes. Jungian, humanistic, and existential psychologists have written extensively about the ability of the psyche to recover from trauma through its recreative capacities, especially by generating centralizing symbols. Jung calls such symbols, which frequently emerge in time of crisis, "constellating" symbols, around which life patterns arrange themselves in new ways. Tremendous relief can come from such reconfiguration of experience; one suddenly feels released from what seemed inescapably reiterative life patterns. By finding a way to tell one's story differently, a sense of possibility is restored, and free will, expressed in the act of authorship, reengages in the old, valiant struggle against fate.

Symbols are not, of course, necessarily to be taken as vessels of absolute truth or insight, but as enablers. A symbol links the creative unconscious with the ordering consciousness. A writer open to such offerings of the unconscious has constant access to new ways of seeing and describing experience. Progoff writes, "A symbol appears as a spontaneous image which emerges from the depth of the personality and acts as a vehicle by which the potentiality latent in the unconscious of the individual can be carried forward. It provides the motive force by which this potentiality can unfold and become actual in the world."[16] This is very close to the modernists' belief in the transformative and enlightening power of the image, best expressed in Pound's words as that which "brings together a complex of feelings and emotions. . . ." Pushed to the limits of rational discourse, writers seize upon images that will bypass the rational faculty and convey the multidimensionality of events and feelngs, healing by direct appeal to imaginative and visceral apprehension. An image thus can initiate healing as well as, conversely, being a product of the healing process as, in the course of remembering, retracing, and revising, memory and imagination converge. In Wiesel's *Night*, for instance, remembered incidents and scenes--a small boy hanging from a scaffold, a dying man crawling toward a soup cauldron, a burning pit--become powerful unifying images that provide an inscape or microcosm of the whole experience described. Memory provides the image; imagination associates the image with all the unpatterned, unarticulated aspects of the experience, and it becomes a center of gravity and a hub of meaning.

The creative and recreative dialogue between conscious and unconscious that the autobiographical act sets into motion inevitably produces conflicts that can themselves become catalysts toward a new stage of assimilation. According to Jung,

> the energy engendered by the tension of the opposites flows into the creation of the symbol, since through the activity of the unconscious a content is brought to life in which thesis and antithesis participate in equal measure--in other words, the birth of the symbol portends a

> reconciliation into a more fully inclusive and comprehending plane of experience . . .[17]

The possibilities inherent in an image establish a direction of growth and a trajectory of narration. Images have, as Progoff puts it, a "life cycle" of their own. As their metaphorical implications unfold, they produce patterns and the patterns disclose themselves through performance. Autobiography is the most direct way of articulating this unfolding process. What emerges in autobiography, therefore, is a symbolic self.

Symbols also comment upon experience. They have an evaluative, as well as a reflective and generative function. The evaluation of experience generally becomes apparent only in the act of consciously interpreting symbols, as when one reflects back upon a dream. The production of meaningful symbols is one phase and the interpretation another--one a writerly the other a readerly function.

Progoff calls the symbols that emerge from the unconscious to give us guidance in interpreting experience "formative symbols." He claims that they have a special importance in "releasing tremendous amounts of energy for directed action."[18] When the symbolic dimension of existence opens itself to an individual, his view of reality is strikingly changed. He is able, by means of the symbol, to perceive things simultaneously on different levels--to unify experience through it. The symbol thus functions in much the same way as Pound described the function of the "image"--to bring together a complex of ideas and emotions in non-discursive fashion, making possible a more holistic comprehension of experience than is expressible in linear discourse.

Though the usefulness of images or symbols lies precisely in their nonlinguistic or prelinguistic character, articulation in language completes the process they initiate. Coordinating image with idea, symbol with syntax, is the next stage in the autobiographical process. If an image or symbol seems highly suggestive, that suggestiveness demands to be made explicit. The process of making explicit is dialectical; the way the symbol surfaces from the unconscious tends to preclude mere imposition of idea upon experience and invites a more organic process of "unfolding" as "ideas and images seem to find each other."[19]

The aim remains wholeness. As temporal creatures, of course, we are never entirely whole. Time consistently presses us forward, from one incompletion to another. Yet though the ideal of wholeness may be illusory, it seems to be necessary to make sense of existence. We need to experience physical and spiritual integrity. And one way to assure ourselves of that integrity is to shape experience in writing, giving it comprehensible contours and boundaries. We need, moreover, not only to experience integrity within ourselves, but also to become part of a larger whole. Wholeness means both inner coherence and connection with a community--ultimately with the cosmos. Stephen Spender sees autobiography thus as the author's "plea for humanity to relate his isolation to its wholeness."[20] This plea is the more urgent as social alienation reaches epidemic proportions.

The pursuit of wholeness can easily become reductive, however. Autobiography can become facile and false if it is used to reduce the complexities of experience to a set of conventions or to articulate a single dominant moral theme. Indeed the romantic ideal of wholeness is in some ways incompatible with modern sensibility.[21] Surely if any single notion of reality might be used to characterize "modern sensibility" it would be fragmentation and dissonance rather than integration and wholeness.

As a form, autobiography resists perfectedness, since a life story must remain uncompleted. But crisis narratives can achieve closure--one can say, "Now the crisis is past"--and life goes on. The danger in seeking wholeness is the temptation to create a false unity, one that turns life into a static work of art. When autobiography succumbs to this compulsion a means of growth turns into an elaborate defense mechanism, enclosing and fixing rather than expanding the parameters of the life story. This can happen when control supersedes insight--when imposition of pattern upon experience overtakes the delicate process of discovery and recognition that the autobiographical act can catalyze. The true function of autobiography is not to force memories into symbolic patterns, but to discern whatever principles of integrity survive life crises and to clarify those principles in such a way that they become centering points for reconstructing the world.

Revision and Regeneration

Healing is completed in transformation. As a writer gains distance from personal crisis, the opportunities for artful revision of autobiographical material become clearer. In autobiographical fiction, an author can actually finish an experience, reach a conclusion, reclaim the past and build on it. The process is dialectical: in his or her writing the author enters into multiple dialogues--between the conscious and the unconscious, between inner and outer voices, between the living self and the emerging text.

When Progoff shifted the psychotherapeutic process from talking in a clinical setting to writing in a private journal, he continued to emphasize the dialectical aspect of healing by formatting each section of the prescribed journal as a structured dialogue. Thus the journal replicated the essential therapeutic pattern of description and interpretive response. His technique reveals how many simultaneous voices can be activated within the individual, and enter that dialogue. His hypothesis is that by allowing those voices to speak, individuals can tap resources of wisdom within themselves that they were not fully aware of, as well as separate their essential "selves" from the self-destructive elements in their psyches, and, in a very real way, become agents of their own healing.

Progoff emphasizes that an important part of journal work is the process of "feedback" or "reading oneself" by reading what one has written about oneself. Often we don't see things until we express them: W.H. Auden's famous question--"How can I know what I think till I see what I say?"-aptly characterizes this truth. Reading, therefore, is an integral part of the autobiographical act. Janet Varner Gunn calls the autobiographer the "paradigmatic reader" of his own work--a "reader of his or her self" engaged in the act of interpretation almost simultaneously with the act of creation.[22] And in interpretation lies much of healing: the object of telling dreams to a therapist is to get help in interpreting the symbolic signals that come as gifts from the unconscious for guidance and healing, through them to gain direction and derive strategies for changing one's life. The autobiographer, therefore, always plays a double role: he or she is both subject and object, both patient and healer, both the writer of his life and the reader of it. Indeed, Geoffrey Hartman has suggested that the act of writing *is* an act of reading, the two being simply different aspects of the merging processes of selection, organization, and revision.[23]

The transforming moment in this dialectical process comes when new questions emerge that call not only upon memory, but upon imagination: What might this situation look like from a different angle? What could I have changed? What opportunities has this experience created? How can I make it accessible to readers? These are questions that can lead ultimately to the making of fiction.

For an autobiography to be rewritten as fiction, the author must take a new look at the past and reassess its possibilities. The task is no longer excavation, but building upon the foundation of experience. Wiesel's *Night* and Brittain's *Testament of Youth* were both followed by works of fiction that probed and elaborated the meaning of the memories recorded in those autobiographies. The fictional works were variations on central autobiographical themes, expanding their implications like widening ripples as the therapeutic impulse gradually gave way to broader artistic and social concerns.

The relationship between therapy and art is not, however, simply sequential, but remains a complex interaction at any stage. One early critic of autobiography claimed that to the extent that a piece of writing is therapeutic it is not artistic--that true art must be purified of the self-reflexive motive.[24] While such dogma seems simplistic, it does seem that the artistic and the therapeutic constitute poles of a critical spectrum, and that, with proper qualifications, locating literary works along this spectrum can contribute a great deal to our understanding of their significance. Furthermore, this spectrum may provide a useful analogue to the stages a writer goes through in emerging from crisis.

A person in crisis is immersed, trapped "inside" his or her experience. The metaphor of emergence expresses the need to "get outside" the experience in order to regain perspective and control. As Janet Varner Gunn points out, the autobiographer's own life is often "so close to him that he cannot see it . . . simply not strange enough to be grasped."[25] Writing can effect a necessary estrangement; the authorial stance places one "outside" an experience, and at a vantage point from which one can give it syntax, shape, and structure. Language in its way enables us to become agents rather than victims of circumstance--to enact rather than simply to suffer change. Writing begun as therapy will, continued, tend toward art. Therapy is the beginning of healing; art can be its completion.

[1] Max Frisch, *Montauk* (New York: Harcourt, Brace, Jovanovich, 1976), Introduction.

[2] Anais Nin, "The Personal Life Deeply Lived," in Albert E. Stone, *The American Autobiography* (Englewood Cliffs, NJ: Prentice-Hall, Inc., 1981), p. 161.

[3] Carl Jung, *Memories, Dreams, and Reflections* , trans. Richard and Clara Winston (New York: Random House, 1963), pp. vi-vii.

[4] Kenneth Burke, *The Philosophy of Literary Form* (Berkeley: University of California Press, 1973), pp. 293 ff.

[5] Langdon Elsbree, *The Rituals of Life: Patterns in Narratives* (Port Washington, NY: National University Publications, 1982), p. 11.

[6] Richard Church, "The Art of Autobiography," *Cornhill* 171 (1960-61), p. 479.

[7] Alfred Kazin, "The Self as History: Reflections on Autobiography," in Albert Stone, *The American Autobiography* (Englewood Cliffs, NJ: Prentice-Hall, Inc., 1981), p. 41.

[8] Laura Marcus, "Autobiography and Psychoanalysis," paper presented at 1983 convention of the Modern Language Association, New York, p. 1.

[9] Ira Progoff, *At a Journal Workshop* (New York: Dialogue House Library, 1975), p. 24.

[10] Louis Renza, "The Veto of the Imagination: A Theory of Autobiography" in James Olney, *Autobiography: Essays Theoretical and Critical* (Princeton: Princeton University Press, 1980), pp. 84-114.

[11] Jonathan Culler, *Structuralist Poetics: Structuralism, Linguistics and the Study of Literature* (Ithaca, NY: Cornell University Press, 1975), introduction.

[12] James Olney, "Autobiography and the Cultural Moment" in Olney, p. 11.

13 Janet Varner Gunn, *Autobiography: Toward a Poetics of Experience* (Philadelphia: University of Pennsylvania Press, 1982), p. 33.

14 Carl Jung, *Aion: Researches into the Phenomenology of the Self* (Princeton: Princeton University Press, 1959), p. 3.

15 Carl Jung, *Psyche and Symbol* , ed. Violet de Laszlo (New York: Doubleday Books, 1958), pp. 30-31.

16 Ira Progoff, *The Symbolic and the Real* (New York: Julian Press, Inc., 1963), p. 23.

17 Progoff, *Symbolic*, p. 94.

18 Progoff, *Symbolic*, p. 71.

19 William Howarth, "Some Principles of Autobiography," in Olney, p. 111.

20 Stephen Spender, "Confession and Autobiography," in Olney, p. 120.

21 J.P. Riquelme, "The Unspeakable 'I' of Modernism: From Yeats to Beckett." Paper presented at the 1983 convention of the Modern Language Association, New York, p. 2.

22 Gunn, p. 68.

23 Geoffrey Hartman, *Criticism in the Wilderness* (New Haven: Yale University Press, 1980), pp. 19-20.

24 Roy Pascal, *Design and Truth in Autobiography* (Cambridge, MA: Harvard University Press, 1960), pp. 91 ff.

25 Gunn, p. 74.

CHAPTER 2

REMEMBERING AND IMAGINING

The Dangers of Remembering

One common experience autobiographers describe is fear of remembering. The urge to explore the past competes with a powerful urge to escape it, particularly if that past is filled with anguish. Memories may come unbidden, but when they come, one can decide whether to resist them or enter into them--whether to stay on the surface or to plunge into the past and become vulnerable again to recollected suffering. Remembering is a decision.

In her poem, "Diving into the Wreck," Adrienne Rich offers an apt metaphor for the autobiographer's task.1 Once crisis is past and the vestiges mercifully buried under obscuring layers of intervening time, it takes an act of exceptional courage, and a strong need, to risk reopening old wounds, reawakening old confusions, reviving old agonies, returning to the scene of old failures and losses. Remembering is dangerous.

"I came to explore the wreck," Rich writes. "I came to see the damage that was done." Still at the surface, before the dive, she can look from a position of safety down into the depths at the wreckage she once inhabited. Once she was a victim, in danger of drowning. Now, a survivor, she can make the dive to explore the wreck, prepared to return unharmed, but dangers remain. She outfits herself with equipment to keep from drowning: "The body-armor of black rubber, / the absurd flippers,/ the grave and awkward mask." She is equipped for exploration as well as for survival, having "read the book of myths,/ and loaded the camera, and checked the knife-blade" She is prepared to see and interpret, to extract and retrieve, to survive in the depths for a time, and ultimately to escape.

The dive must be undertaken alone. She must learn, she says, "alone to turn my body without force in the deep element," submitting to the different conditions that prevail under the surface, relinquishing a measure of control. Leaving behind the safety of sunlight and air, she lets go of all securities but the few she can carry with her, and descends to the rotting wreck.

The diver not only looks upon the "ribs of disaster," scanning the familiar shape of the decaying hull with her light beam, but enters the hold, penetrating to the darkest, most threatening place. The danger of her situation increases as the poem builds to the moment of confrontation when she surveys it from within and sees: "the thing I came for: the wreck and not the story of the wreck the thing itself and not the myth . . ." This is the difference between whole remembering and mere "remembering that." The view from the surface is very different from full immersion in the past.

The dangers are multiple. A diver must be both daring and cautious, and must be skilled and fit for the task. Language is her enabler. "The words are purposes. / The words are maps." Words in the "book of myths" give her some guidance; words of the poem reshape the experience of remembering when she returns from the dive, carrying the "book of myths / in which / our names do not appear." To get to "the thing itself," she needed the book of myths, but having descended into the wreck and seen it with her own eyes, myths fall away and are replaced by words which express a private vision that is actual. The deepest kind of memory is this moment of vision, this experience of "being there."

This experience is not for everyone. Descending into the past and the depths of the self is a perilous journey, not to be undertaken lightly. In her essay on modernist autobiography, R.V. Arana points out the gravity of the "autobiographic risk"--the autobiographer, she says, confronts "the problem of facing one's inner demons, the monsters that drive one to the brink, or over the brink, into insanity."[2] Returning to the things which drove one to the edge of despair or madness can take one there again, out to that falling-off place. The danger of losing objectivity, of drowning by reimmersion, is real. Curiosity and nostalgia are not enough.

Jung emphasizes the risk of such an undertaking in his own autobiography, *Memories, Dreams, and Reflections* , where he writes of his experimental journeys into the unconscious and the collective past:

> In order to grasp the fantasies which were stirring in me 'underground,' I knew that I had to let myself plummet down into them, as it were. I felt not only violent resistance to this, but a distinct fear. For I was afraid of losing command of myself and becoming prey to the fantasies--and as a psychiatrist I realized only too well what that meant.[3]

Only a driving need to understand, a need to make peace with ghosts that continue to haunt, or a deep sense of vocation are sufficient motivation for this task.

Elie Wiesel is one autobiographer who knows well both the urgent need to remember and the dangers it entails. To return again and again to memories of Auschwitz is to engage in an ongoing struggle with despair, and is an invitation to madness. Either would be a commensurate response. Wiesel knows at the outset that there will be no grail at the end of his quest: there are no satisfactory answers to the questions raised by the Holocaust. He believes nevertheless that the risks must be taken and the journey made so that the past will not be buried in obscurity and consequently repeated. The dangers of remembering must be undertaken to avert the greater dangers of forgetting.

Remembering must be conducted with care and the right intention if it is not to result in paralysis, he claims, recalling the fate of Lot's wife who looked back and turned into a piller of salt:

> And Lot's apprehensive wife, she was right to want to look back and not be afraid to carry the burning of doomed hope. 'Know where you come from,' the sages of Israel said. But everything depends on the inner attitude of whoever looks back to the beginning: if he does so purely out of intellectual curiosity, his vision will make of him a statue in some salon.[4]

For Wiesel, as for Rich, words are "purpose" and "maps." In the absence of his earlier faith in transcendent things, faith in language is a saving grace. "Language can mend anything," he says--though not without irony, knowing too well how it can also destroy.[5] While recognizing that many of the atrocities of the Holocaust were carried out by means of language--labels, euphemisms, propaganda--he recognizes also that language has as powerful a capacity to regenerate as to destroy. His preparation for the journey into the past is to select carefully from among the words available to him, and make those words weapons against the words that destroy. But words are, as Eliot put it, "shabby equipment, always deteriorating," and Wiesel knows this. He only uses them for lack of anything better, because he does not know how to speak with silence: "If I could . . . communicate a Silence through silence I would do so," he told one interviewer. "But I cannot. Perhaps I am not strong enough or wise enough. I try to communicate that Silence with words."[6] Their very inadequacy impresses upon him more and more deeply how hopeless is the task of telling the tale he has survived to tell. To find the right words he makes himself vulnerable to the pain, immersing himself in it in order to renew its immediacy.

In *Testament of Youth* Brittain, like Wiesel, undertook to reenter her "shattered youth" by means of words that she knew to be inadequate, driven, like him, by a sense of calling:

> I make no apology for the fact that some of these documents renew with fierce vividness the stark agonies of my generation in its early twenties. The mature proprieties of 'emotion remembered in tranquillity' have not been my object, which, at least in part, is to challenge that too easy, too comfortable relapse into forgetfulness which is responsible for history's most grievous repetitions. (12)

She, too, "dove into the wreck," trying to get past obscuring myths and confront the "thing itself" in order to come to some healing vision of her past that would reveal a new and needed truth about it. Autobiography seemed an obvious and proper means:

> Only, I felt, by some . .. attempt to write history in terms of personal life could I rescue something that might be of value, some element of truth and hope and usefulness, from the smashing up of my own youth by the war. (11)

Going back, for Brittain, involved not only contemplation of the huge personal losses of the war years, but of the losses the intervening years had brought as well: loss of the passionate intensity she recognized in her journal, of the capacity for hopefulness that sustained her then, and of an irrecoverable innocence that, while it offered her little protection against shattering disillusionments, gave her a spiritual vitality hard to regain. Despair, bitterness, resentment and disappointment endangered the detachment and balance required for the documentary reconstruction she attempted.

Like Wiesel, Brittain had lost faith in transcendent meaning, and looked to the secular world and to language to provide some perspective that would make the past useful and render it less threatening. But the struggle with language itself is not an easy one, and has its own dangers. Autobiography became, for them both, a kind of double jeopardy.

The multiple hazards of reentering the past to write about it are equally evident in Robert Pirsig's searching autobiographical inquiry into his own mental history. Having virtually lost contact, through electroshock therapy, with his brilliant but erratic pre-psychotic self, he ventured from the distance of a decade to approach and chart the inner territory where he had once become hopelessly lost. Thomas Couser notes how dangerous it was for Pirsig to revisit the scene of his mental breakdown:

> The reconstruction of Phaedrus's intellectual system holds certain dangers for Pirsig. To follow Phaedrus is to risk getting lost in 'the high country of the mind'--to

> lose touch with concrete things and other people.7

In order successfully to reenter that threatening frame of reference, Pirsig had to find a narrative stance that was simultaneously vulnerable and protected--to be both receptive and resistant to the ghost of his former self. Madness is an insidious seduction. He had to find a way to identify with Phaedrus and yet remain separate from him. The solution to his problem lay in devising a narrative form that enabled him to alternate between two realities, anchored in the present story of his journey while exploring the uncharted implications of his shrouded past. The book simultaneously describes two kinds of journeys: the narrative of his motorcycle trip with his son, Chris, parallels his solitary journey into the past. Each has its own dangers, frustrations, and exhilarations. Pirsig's difficulties in communicating with his son on that trip mirror ironically the difficulties he had as Phaedrus communicating with the world at large. Chris becomes a foil, a measure of Pirsig's normality, and his anchor in the "real world" as he makes his repeated dives into Phaedrus's mental universe.

Christa Wolf uses a similar device in *A Model Childhood*. She takes her daughter, Lenka, with her to the little Polish town where she grew up, returning to search for the self who lived her formative years under Hitler, trying to make connection with a past she has tried heretofore to reject. "What is past is not dead," she writes. "It is not even past. We cut ourselves off from it; we pretend to be strangers" (3). Her daughter's barbed questions, incredulous horror and uninformed judgments characterize the seeing from the outside, while the narrator herself tries to enter her own memories from the inside, to enter the hold of the wreck and remember what it was like to dwell there. It is a painful, humbling process. She accuses herself:

> You abandoned the child, after all. After others abandoned it. All right, but she was also abandoned by the adult who slipped out of her, and who managed to do to her all the things adults usually do to children. The adult left the child behind, pushed her aside, forgot

> her, suppressed her, denied her, remade, falsified, spoiled and neglected her, was ashamed and proud of her, loved her with the wrong kind of love, and hated her with the wrong kind of hate. Now, in spite of all impossibility, the adult wishes to make the child's acquaintance. (7)

Rather than suffer a crippling amputation of her past, she seeks to forge a stronger connection with it, finding the threads that link then with now, redeeming the past in light of the present, to use and control it, and thereby end its threat.

But memories produce more memories. Once opened, the Pandora's box of memory cannot be easily closed. In her narrative, Wolf discloses the alternations between authorial control and threatening memories that come upon her unbidden and demand attention. She realizes that she must be prepared for these surprise attacks by her ghosts. The dangers of her search are not all predictable. As has often been observed, writers write, in part, "to discover what they have to say." That discovery is often startling and threatening, and takes them into places they had not planned to enter.

Though his journey into the past is only figural, C.S. Lewis, in *A Grief Observed*, describes an odyssey of grief similar to Wolf's in its ambiguities. Grief, too, is immersion in memory, and a struggle to accept the "pastness of the past" and endure its continuing presence. Grief, he writes, "is like a long valley, a winding valley." In the process of recording his grief and exploring his memories, Lewis becomes aware of several dangers--or, as he views them, temptations--that lie like snares along his path. One of these dangers is sentimentality--nostalgia that falsifies the past and would keep him entrapped in fruitless longing for what cannot return. He realizes that he is longing for something that never was--that sentimentality tends to create idealized versions of the past. He is wary of the deceptions of wishful thinking that sidetrack him as he seeks to retrieve something from his great loss. "The reality is no longer there to check me," he writes, "to pull me up short, as the real H. so often did, so unexpectedly, by being so thoroughly herself and not me. . . . The rough, sharp, cleansing tang of her otherness is gone" (20, 22). He observes the tendency of memory to soften outlines, to blur, and to make the world of the past into an extension of desire. If not disciplined, memory will, he fears, turn her into an imaginary woman to tempt him into self-indulgent fantasies rather than preserving that about her which was vital and corrective:

> Slowly, quietly, like snow-flakes--the snow flakes that come when it is going to snow all night--little flakes of me, my impressions, my selections, are settling down on the image of her. The real shape will be quite hidden in the end. . . . genuine and wholly involuntary memories can still, thank God, at any moment rush in and tear the strings out of my hands. But the fatal obedience of the image, its insipid dependence on me, is bound to increase. (22, 24)

Not only the falsehoods of sentimentality, but the self-centeredness they foster dismay him.

Another form of self-indulgence Lewis recognizes as a danger is the perverse vanity that feeds upon grief--the tendency to resist recovery and to make himself into a tragic hero. What he calls the "bath of self-pity, the wallow, the loathsome stickysweet pleasure of indulging it" disgusts him. He gives these emotional states harsh names to warn himself against their debilitating effects. He describes these dangers or temptations in the bluntest terms, as if to remind himself of their grotesqueness. He uses epithets like "maudlin tears," "filth and nonsense" like sharp sword-thrusts at the illusions grief fosters.

One by one, Lewis singles out possible ways in which he might succumb to grief and tells himself, in effect, "This I will not do." His attempts to understand the psychology of grief reveal a deep fear of being crippled, diminished, or degraded by it. He sees grief as a disease which threatens to destroy the healthy contact with reality that is sanity. He fears weakness and self-indulgence to the point of becoming extraordinarily judgmental of his own emotions. His weakened state subjects him to sicknesses of the soul. Grief, he believes, does not ennoble, but weakens, and must be confronted as a temptation. Thus his observations return repeatedly to the questions, What is grief doing to me? What are the dangers in it that I must be aware of? What might it make of me? Naming is his means of control: if he can name the dangers to which he is vulnerable, he can, he hopes, better avoid them.

For all these writers, reentering the past is a daring act of self-exposure and a leap of faith, like the "credo ut intelligam" which Janet Varner Gunn claims is "paradigmatic of all acts of autobiography."[8] Their narratives are logs of the deep sea journey into the wreck, efforts to find "the thing itself and not the myth" by letting go of the protective conventions they live by, realizing that, as Wolf says, "the past is not dead; it is not even past."

Holding On and Letting Go

In *A Model Childhood*, Wolf describes a dream she had in the course of writing her autobiography. In the dream she saw her book before her--"the fat book into which years of your life are entering. Which you want and at the same time don't want." Writing it, she reflects, is like "driving with the brakes on. Bad for the motor" (348). Ambivalence and hesitation are predictable responses to reopening closed doors to the past. Bringing painful memories into consciousness engages one in a struggle for sanity and hope. No wonder many autobiographers "drive with one foot on the brake"--in his or her paradoxical quest the autobiographer is often pursuing something he or she may not want to find, constantly tempted by what Wolf calls "the mortal sin of our time: the desire not to come to grips with oneself" (406). In the course of writing the writer must constantly decide what to pursue and what to avoid, risking presumption on the one hand, bad faith on the other. He or she must establish a direction in a wilderness of memories, and find some principle of selection that will indicate what to include and exclude, what to keep, examine, and let go. Motives shift as the sense of vulnerability deepens. Active curiosity and even longing often give way to dread and resistance.

Autobiographical writing can be described in the same way Freud described the process of remembering: Freud himself pointed out the similarity between the acts of remembering and writing.[9] Just as the effort to remember conflicts with the impulse to repress, autobiographical writing generally proceeds from two apparently contradictory impulses: the impulse to preserve the past and the equally powerful urge to be rid of it. Yeats surely spoke for many autobiographers when he observed that writing about the past gives one a way to "begin to forget it all."[10] The metaphors autobiographers use to describe the processes of remembering and writing reflect this tension between opposed objectives. They speak of preserving, salvaging, redeeming, and resurrecting, but also of "writing out" the past--purging it, laying it to rest, bringing it to closure. Writing which "gets down" the memories also "gets them out." The autobiographical risk, or leap of faith, is generally accompanied by deliberate self-protective strategies. Derrida claims, in fact, that "there is no writing which does not devise some protection, *to protect against itself* , against the writing by which the 'subject' is himself threatened as he lets himself be written: as he *exposes himself.*"[11] These two impulses, to create and to conserve, express themselves in two essentially different attitudes toward the past. Riquelme distinguishes these attitudes as metaphoric and ironic--the first essentially Romantic, and the second modernist. To metaphorize is to reclaim by transforming. To ironize is, at least in part, to disclaim or dismiss.

A Grief Observed offers a clear example of the use of metaphor as a conservative strategy. In the journal Lewis finds in writing a way to let go of his wife in one form to regain her in another. This transformation is only possible through language and images. There is no one for him to hold on to, but he discovers as he writes new ways of bringing her to consciousness that figuratively restore her in a way that is not morbid, but heartening:

> 'She is in God's hand.' That gains a new energy when I think of her as a sword. Perhaps the earthly life I shared with her was only part of the tempering. Now perhaps

> He grasps the hilt; weighs the new weapon; makes lightnings with it in the air. 'A right Jerusalem blade.' (73)

Metaphor makes change tolerable to him. The image of the sword captures the qualities in her he cherished most: sharpness, strength, and endurance. Almost playfully, he finds other metaphors that bring her back in other ways. He writes, for instance, that she is "like a nest of gardens, wall within wall, hedge within hedge, more secret, more full of fragrant and fertile life, the further you entered" (73). Remembering her as a garden allows him to wander among his memories peacefully, appreciatively, as one at home among plants he has tended. He focuses upon her being, not upon the loss of her. In a single poetic act he lets go of her and finds her again, and is no longer quite so tormented, but able to be comforted by the thought of her.

Entertaining and elaborating such images allows one both to hold on and to let go. An autobiographical text is a record of what has been preserved, rescued from the sea of memory. What was lost is restored in a different form, and also relinquished, bringing relief and freedom from the torment of unarticulated memories.

In *Testament of Youth* Brittain attests to the pull of similarly opposing desires. Her ambivalence about her vanished world is everywhere apparent. At times her reminiscences are tinged with nostalgia for a pastoral pre-war life, but more often she looks back upon that time as one of restriction, frustrating limitations, and dangerous illusions. She sees herself as having grown up in a "provincial prison" in which she felt "trammeled and trapped." In such an environment, she observes, boys and girls were "easy victims . . . for the war propagandist," with their "naive, uninformed generosities and enthusiasms"(49). And she concludes that such provincialism now seems to her "the sum total of all false values" (55). Yet while she deplores the blindness in which she and her generation were raised, Brittain finds that in fact some of the tastes and values apparently least relevant to survival helped her to survive. That period of innocence had, she admits, a role in shaping her destiny that was not altogether weakening and destructive. "It is arguable," she reflects, "that our early months of illumined faith were a factor in the ultimate return of some of us to life"(38).

Even Brittain's period of deep grief is a part of her past toward which she is ambivalent. She acknowledges the temptation to cling to grief and prolong mourning, remembering how long she did so after Roland's death. When people assured her that time would heal, she recalls,

> I resented the suggestion bitterly. I could not believe it, and did not even want it to be true. If time did heal I should not have kept faith with Roland, I thought, clinging assiduously to my pain, for I did not then know that if the living are to be of any use in this world, they must always break faith with the dead. (247)

The book is her way of keeping faith, not by grieving, but by making Roland's story, and her continuing life, "useful." At a time shortly after the war when she seriously considered suicide, she resisted it partly by resolving, if she could not be happy, at least to be useful. In the autobiography she "rescued" usable fragments from the heap of broken images the war left in its wake--excerpts from documents from the war years, letters, diaries, news bulletins, poems--and imbedded them in the matrix of an organizing narrative structure, shaping them into a coherent, complex and ironic story of survival.

But Brittain had another objective: she needed to be done with the *Testament* in order to write other things. She tried at first to put the autobiographical material into a novel, but came to feel that only by telling her "true story" directly and starkly could she fulfill her obligation to bear witness. "I knew," she writes in her forward, "that until I had tried to contribute to [a greater understanding of the war] I could never write anything in the least worthwhile"(11). Autobiography was the fulfillment of an obligation she felt to herself, to the dead, and to the post-war generations. It was her duty, as she saw it, to help prevent another of "history's most grievous repetitions" by offering a stark, personal, and "feminine" view of the war as a corrective to the deceptive propaganda that still formed public opinion. Once that was written, she would be released to write other things. Like many other autobiographers, Brittain followed her autobiography with fiction that developed similar themes and reworked the same life experiences. Once written out, she could loosen the hold those memories had upon her, return to them less urgently, less painfully, without a suffocating sense of obligation. Preserving them for the public, she at the same time purged herself of them: like donating relics to a museum, she gave them a wider audience, made them useful, and relieved herself of an onerous responsibility.

The same conviction that one must preserve memories almost too horrible to contemplate, was, of course, Wiesel's primary motivation in publishing an account of his months at Auschwitz. One critic has pointed out that what marks Wiesel and all the protagonists of his novels is "their willing assumption of their past, which includes their wounds."[12] "Assuming" the past means, in Wiesel's case, two things: reaffirming his deep roots in Jewish tradition, and committing himself to remembering the desecrations and humiliations he and his people underwent. His autobiography is an act of commitment to those memories: ironic, ambivalent, and double-edged in places, yet earnest and powerful. He preserves and celebrates his Jewishness despite a fundamental loss of faith, holding onto the memory of pain despite the pain it costs to do so is his way of keeping faith.

But Wiesel also let go of a great deal as he crafted his book. The first draft of *Night* was nearly 1000 pages long; the final version is barely over 100. Distillation and exclusion heighten the significance of what he saved: each image becomes a resonating symbol--a defining instance that represents much more experience than it describes. The work is shaped as much by what is left out as by what is kept; in keeping with his desire to "speak silence," he makes its silences an effective counterpoint to the words of the story.

Unlike Wiesel, Wolf does not present an arrangement of memories, but documents the process of remembering. *A Model Childhood* is a book about remembering in which the author imitates in narrative form the way memories surface and engage the writer in often painful confrontation. What the author remembers is loss, disillusionment, and guilt. She takes her difficult journey back into the war years by means of an actual journey back to the scenes of her childhood and youth. She goes in order to find the "child that is hiding"; guilt has led her to disclaim her past. Now she seeks to reclaim it and understand it. She returns to her home town in East Prussia, now Poland, as a "memory test," exposing herself to scenes that will call up memories she had buried. But she does not trust memory; she wants to find a way to discern and hold on to what is "authentic," realizing at the same time that much of what she remembers is partly imagined. She wants to find what relation the person she was bears to the person she now is. "How did we become what we are?" is the question that directs her search. In making that clear, she hopes not only to rediscover but to reunite herself with the child that she was.

At the same time she wants to let go of that child that haunts her--to demystify and exorcise the past. The writing is an attempt to assuage her "survival guilt" by an honest search into motives and causes. It is an answer to the accusing look in her daughter's astonished eyes as Wolf tells her about concentration camps, the bigotry of local merchants, the biology books with their lessons on racial purity. When is innocence culpable? Wolf looks for an answer by examining her own period of strange innocence. "Apparently I had been living in a dictatorship for twelve years without knowing it," she writes wryly. That ironic note is the other side of forgiveness: if her story is an admission of guilt, it is also an act of self-absolution. Only by forgiving herself, she realizes, can she reclaim herself.

This paradoxical act is similar to Pirsig's reuniting himself with the ghost of his past self in order to exorcise it. Haunted by the ghost of "Phaedrus," Pirsig hunts him down in order to reclaim what he recognizes and values in Phaedrus and, by making him other, to reject the insidious temptation to become Phaedrus again. Pirsig describes himself to his son as a man who "spent his whole life hunting for a ghost," but later declares that the purpose of his hunt for Phaedrus was "to bury him-- forever"(60). He gives his ghost a voice in order ultimately to silence him, and by doing so brings the thing that has most threatened his sanity under his authorial control. The more articulated Phaedrus becomes on the page, the less capable he is of dominating the author's consciousness. Both Wolf and Pirsig, seeking to make friends with former selves that they had rejected, turned their secrets into stories. By doing so they became channels rather than vessels, allowing those stories to leave them and flow into the wide public domain.

Remembering Now

A Model Childhood is ridden with self-reflexive questioning that invites the reader to ponder the dynamics of memory and composition. As the writer retraces her past she asks herself, What do I remember? Why those things? Why do some memories appear spontaneously and others need to be dredged up? Why at this point in time? How do I gain access to the person I was? How did I become what I am? The narrative makes a technique of self-consciousness, and richly illustrates John Sturrock's observation that,

> if autobiography is to progress . . . it requires a revaluation less of the past than of the present, of the moment of writing. . . . The autobiographical contract between writer and reader surely has a clause which says that the writer is addressing us from the moment of writing, not from the moments he is remembering.13

Wolf is concerned, as all autobiographers are, with what Eliot called "the presence of the past." If the text is a search for the roots of blindness and of change, she made that search in order to understand the enormous shifts of outlook that transformed her. For the sake of integrity, she needed to reclaim the past self that she had rejected, and to be reconciled with herself as that other. The real subject of *A Model Childhood*, therefore is not "Nelly"--the remembered child--but the "I" who tells the story--the survivor.

Wolf makes a distinction between "the dead, the surviving, and the living." Survivors are not "living" as long as they are governed by guilt over the mere fact of survival. To be among the living she has had to come to terms with the "survival guilt" she feels as a German who participated, however naively, in Hitler's atrocities. She recalls a question from the audience at one of her public readings: "And do you believe it's possible to come to grips with the events that you write about?" and her answer is, "No. (The deaths of six million Jews, twenty million Russians, six million Poles.)" (334) Nevertheless, she is impelled to make the attempt. The autobiography asks what the past has to do with the present. Who she is cannot be assessed until she comes to terms with who she was.

But if the past informs the present, the present also changes the past, and autobiography enacts the changing of the past. In the narrative, present concerns and values become a lens through which the past is viewed. The deep contingency of the autobiographical reconstruction upon the circumstances in which the autobiographer writes is aptly expressed in Barrett Mandel's comment that as

> [the autobiographer's] present needs change his past, whatever interpretation of the same data he may have had in moments preceding the writing of the autobiography will have disappeared forever as he writes 'now.'[14]

The opening sentence of *Testament of Youth*, for instance, establishes at once a vast difference between the Vera Brittain of 1914 and the writer who speaks in the text--one a young woman to whom contemporary political life meant little and seemed remote, the other a speaker for the League of Nations, an active feminist, a fully committed member of the political community. The distance between the two selves is the trajectory traced by the narrative. As her experiences led her directly to her present convictions, those present convictions form a lens that focuses and shapes her memories, and puts the past to use as evidence for her cause.

Writing the autobiography fulfilled a desire that Brittain traces back a long way. A letter she wrote Roland in 1913 reveals how important writing was for her even then, and how deeply rooted the autobiographical impulse:

> I keep getting moments of fierce desire to write something. I don't mind what, except that trifles wouldn't do. Could I write an autobiographical novel, I wonder? Can one make a book out of the very essence of one's self? Perhaps so, if one was left with one's gift stripped bare of all that made it worth having, and nothing else was left... (196)

In the context of the autobiography the irony of these speculations is apparent. Even as she writes she is in the process of answering her own questions. With similar irony she recalls being filled with a desire to write a book about Roland three months after his death, but "concluded that three months was too short a time for me to see personal events in their true perspective." She goes on, "I should have been astonished indeed had anyone told me that I should wait seventeen years" (251). Yet even now she has found that seventeen years fail to provide a "true" perspective.

Brittain realizes that her very need to write, to heal old wounds, necessarily distorts her vision. What she sees at the moment of writing is partly a function of her losses. "One never gets over the loss," she reflects, "for one is never the same after it" (318). The writing in the autobiography arises from present needs, just as the writing in the diaries was a response to the needs of the moment.

Brittain's pervasive irony often presents the relationship of the present to the past in rather bitter fashion. Time failed to obviate her recurrent sense of futility. One particularly ironic passage recalls her return to Oxford after the war:

> Obviously it wasn't a popular thing to have been close to the War; patriots, especially of the female variety, were as much discredited in 1919 as in 1914 they had been honoured. . . . On the whole the 'experience' of those four years didn't seem exactly conducive to the development of a sense of humour--but perhaps I was prejudiced. No doubt the post-war generation was wise in its assumption that patriotism had 'nothing to it,' and we pre-war lot were just poor boobs for letting ourselves be kidded into thinking that it had. The smashing-up of one's youth seemed rather a heavy price to pay for making the mistake, but fools always did come in for a worse punishment than knaves; we knew that now. (490)

Such descriptions of the past are ways of saying, "Now I see." The narrative is infused with tragic irony by which former ignorance is presented in light of painfully acquired vision. She looks back soberly upon moments of desperate hope and reflects,

> How fortunate we were who still had hope, I did not then realize; I could not know how soon the time would come when we should have no more hope, and yet be unable to die. (137)

Brittain's own story and the history of her time are both about surviving the transition from innocence to experience with its accompanying tragic sense of life. Everything is told with a hindsight that conveys a deeply painful sense of what might have been and of the irrevocability of loss. "At that stage of the war," Brittain writes, referring to the early months of conflict, "we were still able to believe that a country which laid down the best of its life would somehow surely find it" (260). The facetious Biblical allusion underscores the impossibility of transcendent hopes in "a world seventeen years older, in which second-rate masculine ability [struggles] helplessly with almost insoluble problems because the first-rate [are] gone from a whole generation (260).

Yet Brittain's irony is not entirely tragic. Irony becomes for her a means of survival and a source of power. Through it she assumes a position of strength in relation to fate. It is a form of negative capability, engendering flexibility, detachment, and even humor. Perceiving and naming radical incongruities, she stands outside them, and when she can do that, she is in control. In the ironic voice that describes her past self, she identifies her present self. She thus seeks both to incorporate her youthful vision and sensibilities and to provide a corrective to them. Conversely, she reexamines her contemporary accounts of those years in order to retrieve their immediacy. Between the two readings of the war she seeks to formulate some redemptive vision of it, however qualified such a redemption might be, and the result is a bifocal view that produces a three-dimensional effect precisely by virtue of its dividedness.

Wiesel's *Night* also invites speculation about the relation of the past to the present. "I know how the tragedy unfolded minute by minute," he writes, "but this knowledge, as if coming from outside, has nothing to do with understanding. There is in all this a portion which will always remain a mystery; a kind of forbidden zone, inaccessible to reason." Wiesel raises not only the question, "How could these things happen?" but also "Could these things still happen?" His opening story about Moche the Beadle, who survived a Gestapo massacre and found, when he returned to warn his town, that no one would believe him, impels the reader to speculate about the resistances in human nature that blind us to what we do not want to see. The event, like many in this story, assumes parabolic universality.

Wolf, likewise ironic about the past, adopts a less authoritative stance. She uses memory less assertively because she trusts it less. "You are hampered," she tells herself, "by unreliable memory" (7). If "I remember" is the autobiographer's main claim to authority, her distrust of memory has the effect of reminding the reader and herself that the present is also an enclosure. Connection with the past is one way out of it, and in *A Model Childhood* she tries to use that connection to enlarge the present, widening her perspective by means of a double vision similar to Brittain's.

By virtue of such widened perspective, the assertion, "I remember," constitutes an indisputable claim to authority. In her analysis of eyewitness documents from the Holocaust, Sidra Ezrahi observes that "the very claim to historicity lends [their] words a certain authority." Furthermore the act of reevaluation implies authority: the autobiographer measures the distance between past and present in order to establish the authority of his or her present interpretation of events. The "Now I see" is especially strong, moreover, in stories of crisis, where the writer has ~emerged" from a period of "immersion" in a situation which he can now begin to judge from "above" or "outside."

Sometimes the act of writing is itself a means of arriving at a judgment and a way of establishing authority. When Rich writes, "I did not know this when I began to write," she is identifying the writing itself as an act of exploration. Writing theorist Donald Murray has called writing "a significant kind of thinking in which the symbols of language assume a purpose of their own and instruct the writer during the composing process."[15] Authorship, in other words, generates authority.

One aim of autobiography, then, is to allow the past to modify the present even as the present reshapes the past. Adrienne Rich calls attention to the nature of this process by the hyphenated term, "re-vision"--a reevaluation of the past in terms of the present which changes both past and present. All autobiography seeks to answer the question, "What are the uses of the past?" Always the writer is looking again, seeing new, and finding new bases for action--in actions already performed whose results are known.

Imagining Back

In his critique of *Zen and the Art of Motorcycle Maintenance*, Thomas Couser makes this salient observation about the role of imagination in autobiography:

> Autobiography is always, in a sense, self-impersonation and self-creation, but this is doubly true of *Zen* , which records episodes in which Pirsig had to imagine his former self in order to create an impression of continuity rather than disjunction between periods of his life. This contributes to the book's fictive feeling; however, Pirsig's role-playing is not in the service of art but of self-discovery and self- preservation.[16]

The autobiographical act is a dialogue between memory and imagination. Phenomenologically the two faculties are similar: the common uncertainty expressed in the question, "Am I remembering or imagining?" suggests how disturbing their confluence sometimes is. The term "imagine" is complicated by a kind of double meaning, since it can imply mistaken perception, as when we say 'He only imagined it.' This notion of imagination as falsification is, of course, the most reductive view of it. In fact, imagining is an integral part of remembering and composing; it generates its own kind of truth in the sense that one cannot be "mistaken" about what one is imagining if, in fact the act of imagining is identified as such.

While autobiography bases its claim to authority on its factuality, it is also true that its significance lies beyond its factual accuracy. Indeed, one critic goes so far as to claim that "it is not so much the history of a life that [autobiographers] are concerned with as what Henry James calls 'the history of . . . imagination.'"[17] Memory speaks in images; when one remembers, fictive and imaginative impulses counterbalance reportorial concern for accuracy. Remembered facts only become autobiography when imagination gives them a shape. Autobiography must therefore be considered a hybrid: a factual mode that relies heavily upon the fictive imagination, bringing memory and imagination together in order to "stabilize the past."

Of course, autobiographers often get their "facts" from second-hand sources. Peter Handke wrote *A Sorrow Beyond Dreams* by piecing together information culled both from his own memories and from stories his mother told, as well as from inferences based on knowledge of her environment. He managed thereby to reconstruct a version of her life story and, in the process, to map his own reactions to the tragedy that ended it.

Some autobiographers find their raw material in contemporary texts--journals, letters, news items. Rich's and Brittain's autobiographical works are essentially "readings" of such texts. Some find "memory aids" by taking journeys to the places where experiences occurred, like Pirsig on his motorcycle journey through Phaedrus's country, or Wolf, who embarks on her journey to Poland as a scavenger archaeologist, hoarding information from any source:

> Memory aids. Lists of names, sketches of the town, scraps of paper with sayings, typical family expressions, proverbs the mother or the grandmother were fond of using, first lines of songs. You started sifting through photographs, which are scarce; the subsequent inhabitants of the house on Soldinerstrasse probably burned the fat brown family album. Not to mention the material readily accessible from books, television, old films: surely not all of it was useless. Just as it isn't useless to sharpen one's focus on 'the present.' (8)

In several passages Wolf records apparently trivial details, like an account of her daily expenditures during a period of a few months after the war. Mundane details like these are the material of reconstruction--they become objects of analysis; they raise questions.

Some autobiographers begin with mental pictures or images, working outward from those into narrative. Wiesel, writing in the loosely connected vignettes that this mode of remembering produces, keeps the image always at the center of the passage, so that the plot becomes a mere setting for an icon that suggests far more than can be said.

Though the imagination can descend into morbid fantasy, the creative, imaginative impulse is generally a sign of health. Often the effect of crisis is to numb the imagination. Wiesel recalls that after the death of his father, which climaxed several nightmare months in Auschwitz, "I felt empty, barren: a useless object, a thing without imagination."18 Journal entries written in a moment of crisis tend to have a cryptic, abbreviated quality, and often tend toward the literal. The return of the elaborative impulse signals what Progoff calls a return of "life-directedness."

One function of the imagination in autobiographical writing is to allow the writer to try out different versions of the self. Patricia Spacks has pointed out that women autobiographers have tended to use the form to "construct virtuous selves, valuing the justification through some *version* of goodness."19 The various versions of the self created are not untrue, except in the most literal sense. Spacks also observes that "words like *image* and *pose* suggest a divergence between the real self and the modes of presenting it, but in fact they may, like *style*, also designate means for communicating self-definition.20

Finding a principle of organization for an autobiography is also an imaginative act. One autobiographer wrote in the 1930's that like many other moderns, he began "to believe that chronological time is an illusion and that some other principle organizes existence."21 The discovery of that organizing principle comes most often from what Wolf would call the "moral imagination." Once a purpose or "use" is defined, facts organize themselves in relation to it, and a new vision of the past emerges. Old categories are questioned and new categories introduced.

It takes a leap of imagination to answer the question, "How do things happen?" It is not simple to describe how events are connected. One can make many different kinds of connections among discrete facts, memories, or images. Often a particular sequence of events can be made to seem inevitable. Some autobiographers deliberately attempt to create this impression; others deliberately subvert it. The process of composition demands, in either case, that one imagine how the events of life are linked. Though any one version falls short of whole truth, every version needs some kind of narrative integrity, some sense of meaningful interrelationship among events and consequences. The search for causality involves imagining back from conclusion to origin. We see this kind of imaginative probing in Handke's narration of his mother's life story--a speculative reconstruction of events, reasoning backward from the suicide to its environmental and psychological causes.

Interpretation is, of course, an essentially imaginative act. The question that inevitably follows crisis: "What did it mean?" invites speculation. Wiesel sees meaning-making as a significant part of the autobiographer's task. "We cannot change events," he reflects, "but we can change meanings. That's our force. We use it and we abuse it."[22] Interpretation not only imparts meaning, but defines relevance. In Wiesel's hands the Judaic tradition of radical reinterpretation became a survival tool. By means of the interpretive imagination, we build upon the past and preserve it. Rich treats interpretation as the main function of autobiography. She uses individual experience as a starting point for the reinterpretation of history, both collective and personal, by imagining a new way of seeing it. Similarly, Brittain's reinterpretation of the mythology of war puts the facts of war experience into a wholly new light.

Finally, the imagination supplements memory through speculation. "What might have been" often becomes the narrative completion of "what has been." Wolf periodically digresses into pure speculation, more candidly than most autobiographers who present everything as pure recollection. She imagines her way into her own mind as a child as she would into the mind of a fictional character she might create: "Nelly may have dreamed dreams of annihilation or of omnipotence, perhaps in alternation" (316) she writes, emphasizing that she memory, like imagination, is a realm of uncertainty, possibility, and inconclusiveness. Autobiographical works like Handke's and Pirsig's bring together "what might have been and what has been." Sometimes this process is unconscious. More often it is highly self-conscious. Handke is quite explicit about his fictionalizing: he begins with what facts he has been able to assemble and proceeds by extrapolation. But as Gusdorf reminds us, admission of the fictive element does not, at least in literary terms, devalue the narrative. Truth is more in the manner of telling than in what is told. As Lawrence Langer observes, "If anything, literature, like all art, is the account of what history has failed to produce on its own, so that men have to step in to make good the deficiency."23

Or, as Eliot put it, "What might have been and what has been/ point to one end which is always present."

Imagining Beyond

Brittain's, Wiesel's, and Wolf's continuations in fiction of the projects they began in autobiography, extrapolating upon personal material, suggest that if memory is rooting, imagination is branching. The movement from reconstructing fact to imagining possibility is part of the regenerative activity that so often follows crisis. First to record, then to interpret, and finally to expand is a pattern many autobiographers follow. When interpretation takes over the data it becomes extrapolation or expansion. Alvin Rosenfeld rather whimsically observes, in his essay on Jewish autobiography: "Indulge imagination and you can have what you will--the riches of magic and mystery, the transforming powers of illusion . . . a momentary triumph over conscience, sense, and time. Omnipotent imagination craves to be indulged and courts indulgence through the wiles of Romance. . ."24 While Rosenfeld goes on to emphasize the danger of distortion through "indulging" the imagination, he also acknowledges its transformative power. The imagination that can make much of little--a story from a few scraps of fact--is a regenerative force. We see such a force vividly at work in Pirsig's autobiography, for example--a long extrapolation upon a few retrieved fragments.

Imagination is another word for hope. The turning point of one of Rich's most hopeful poems, comes with the phrase, "The faithfulness I can imagine . . ." Thus begins a positive vision that follows a long stretch of negatives. When an autobiographer has "come to grips with" the past, decided what to preserve, what to let go of, he or she is free to re-imagine the past, to spin out its implications into further and further branchings. Sometimes this takes a utopian form, with a future thrust, a vision or plan of renewal. Rich, for example, concludes *Of Woman Born* with a reminder that the seeds of renewal and change for women lie in women's imaginations:

> I am convinced that 'there are ways of thinking that we don't yet know about.' I take those words to mean that many women are *even now* thinking in ways which traditional intellection denies, decries, or is unable to grasp. . . . We need to imagine a world in which every women is the presiding genius of her own body. In such a world women will truly create new life, bringing forth not only children . . . but the visions, and the thinking, necessary to sustain, console, and alter human existence--a new relationship to the universe. (290-2)

"This is where we have to begin," she concludes: renewal begins in the imagination.

Sometimes the branching of the imagination leads not into this future orientation, but to varying interpretations or persepctives--an effort to penetrate the past more deeply to mine its implications. Wiesel, for instance, creates a protagonist in *Dawn* (1960), his first novel after *Night*, whose past is similar to his own; he is a concentration camp victim who is now in the position of executioner to a military hostage. Explaining his claim that *Night* was the source for all his other works, Wiesel told an interviewer,

> *Night*, my first narrative, was an autobiographical story, a kind of testimony of one witness speaking of his own life, his own death. . . In each book I explore [one of many possible responses]. In *Dawn* I explore the political action; in *The Accident*, suicide; in *The Town Beyond the Wall*, madness; in *The Gates of the Forest*, faith and friendship; in *A Beggar in Jerusalem*, history, the return. All the stories are one story except

> that I build them in concentric circles. The center is the same and is in *Night*.[25]

Re-imagining the events of one's own life is a process of objectifying, distancing, opening out, branching, creating. The transformative or fictive imagination begins to overtake the reconstructive action of memory. Autobiography becomes no longer primarily archaeological but architectural, as new structures are built upon old foundations.

---

1 Adrienne Rich, "Diving into the Wreck" in Gelpi, ed. *Adrienne Rich's Poems* (New York: W.W. Norton and Co., 1965), pp. 65-68.

2 R. Victoria Arana, "Elegant Intimacy: Monologue and Dialogue in Post World War I Autobiography." Paper presented at the 1983 convention of the Modern Language Association, New York, p. 3.

3 Jung, *Memories* , p. 178.

4 Elie Wiesel, *Legends of Our Time* (New York: Avon Books, 1968), p. 220.

5 Harry J. Cargas, *Harry J. Cargas in Coversation with Elie Wiesel* (New York: Paulist Press, 1976), p. 16.

6 Cargas, p. 5.

7 Couser, p. 188.

8 Gunn, p. 134.

9 Ingrid Stipa, "Remembering and Re-membering the Splintered Self in Rilke's *The Notebooks of Malte Laurens Brigge*." Paper presented at the 1983 convention of the Modern Language Association, New York, p. 11.

10 Riquelme, p. 6.

11 Riquelme, p. 6.

12 Cargas, p. 24.

13 J. Sturrock, "The New Model Autobiographer," *New Literary History*, vol. 9, no. 1, p. 27.

14 Barrett Mandel, "Full of Life Now," in Olney, p. 82.

15 Donald Murray, *Learning Through Teaching* (Montclair, NJ: Boynton/Cook Publishers, 1983), p. 18.

16 Couser, p. 192.

17 John Pilling, *Autobiography and Imagination: Studies in Self-Scrutiny* (London: Routledge and Kegan Paul, 1981), p. 4.

18 Wiesel, *Legends* , p. 19.

19 Patricia Meyer Spacks, "Women's Stories, Women's Selves," *The Hudson Review* 30 (1977), p. 43.

20 Spacks, p. 43.

21 Frank Conroy, *Stop Time* (New York: Penguin Books, 1967), p. 21.

22 Cargas, p. 48.

23 Langer, p. 9.

24 Alvin Rosenfeld, "Inventing the Jew: Notes on Jewish Autobiography" in Albert Stone, *The American Autobiography* (Englewood Cliffs, NJ: Prentice-Hall, Inc., 1981), p. 154.

25 Cargas, p. 86.

CHAPTER 3

SILENCE AND WORDS

Silencing

In *Testament of Youth* Vera Brittain recalls how little voice women had in the shaping of collective destiny during the war; many of those most willing and able to serve who offered their services to the War Office were told "that all that was required of women was to go home and keep quiet (195)". Even as she wrote this, Brittain herself was confronting such silencing in a subtler form. In her introduction to Brittain's *Testament of Experience*, Carolyn Heilbrun recalls:

> Brittain's record of what had happened to her in the larger world of events was not only different, but adjudged insignificant. At the time she wrote *Testament of Youth* nobody supposed that the public would be interested in another war book, let alone a war book by a woman.1

For a woman, authorship was still a difficult and daring act of self-assertion. Women were expected to remain in the private sphere, and most of them did. Autobiography was Brittain's answer to silencing. The authority of an autobiographer is difficult to deny because of the cirucmscribed nature of the authority she claims. The form provided a way for Brittain to give an account of war that challenged the myths and conventions that surrounded it. The book traces not only her deepening consciousness of the evils of war, but also her increasing awareness of the insidious ways in which women had been schooled to betray themselves, to accept various forms of oppression, to discount their own perceptions, and to remain silent.

Rich similarly takes up the issue of the silencing of women in *Of Woman Born* where she analyzes the effects of institutionalized rhetoric that projects categories upon human experience, validating some parts of it and suppressing others. Convention establishes the terms in which we can communicate but thereby also largely determines what experiences are communicable. A zone of silence lies between the normative and the actual--what is prescribed and what is experienced. That zone of silence is the territory Rich seeks to chart in her reflections upon the suppressed areas of suffering in her own life that reiterate an untold story common to many women. "We know," she writes, "that there is another story to be told."[2] "Motherhood--unmentioned in the histories of conquest and serfdom, wars and treaties, exploration and imperialism--has a history . . ." (15). She observes that in published theories of child-rearing, "female sources are rarely cited (yet those sources exist, as the feminist historians are showing); there are virtually no primary sources from women-as-mothers; and all this is presented as objective scholarship" (xix).

Rich begins the task of telling the untold story of women's lives by examining her own memories of young motherhood in a culture that falsified the experience of motherhood and silenced women by making it an object of sentimental piety. She remembers depression, "murderous anger," "the futility of any attempt to salvage myself" (3,5). "For centuries no one talked of these feelings," she writes. "The words are being spoken now, are being written down; the taboos are being broken, the masks of motherhood are cracking through" (5). By breaking through those masks she seeks to connect the silent and suppressed realm of feelings with the carefully composed and acculturated public persona to bring to light unacknowledged realities of her own and other women's lives. She writes, "I don't see radical feminism as proceeding from anything but a connection between inner and outer."[3]

Rich's metaphors for her autobiographical act are violent ones: "I have invaded various professional domains, broken various taboos" (xviii). Breaking out of silence is conceived as an act of violence. Her poem, "The Phenomenology of Anger," concludes with the lines, "Every act of becoming conscious / (it says here in this book) / is an unnatural act."[4] What is "natural," of course, is a matter of definition--and patriarchy has by and large made men the definers and silenced women. By quoting Thoreau here Rich takes issue with the male's tacit assumption of the right to define such key terms as "natural." If women accept the definitions provided in the books men have authored, they abdicate their own authority to define such terms. Rich reclaims that authority for women in this poem and in her autobiography. In these texts she attempts to bring female consciousness to expression and find modes of expression that revise and redefine those provided by male consciousness. Conventional ways of describing experience are strong; and the conventions are predominantly male-oriented. To bring alternative ways of seeing to expression involves justification, redefinition, and revision at every turn. The innumerable tacit assumptions imbedded in the language and forms we use have to be questioned, as the poet does in this poem.

In *Zen and the Art of Motorcycle Maintenance* Pirsig also examines how conventional discourse and categories silence or obscure certain modes of perception. As he goes about reconstructing the vision of the world he held as "Phaedrus," he asks why existing language and categories of thought militated against that vision, forcing him into the intellectual isolation that drove him to insanity. After a long period of silence, Pirsig attempts to come to terms with his "ghost" by lifting his sentence of silence, and articulating the vision for him. Insanity, too, is surrounded with taboos. Although Pirsig believes now as he did then that Phaedrus had something important to say, he recalls,

> no one was listening at that time and they only thought him eccentric at first, then undesirable, then slightly mad, and then genuinely insane. There seems little doubt that he was insane, but much of his writing at the time indicates that what was driving him insane was this hostile opinion of him. Unusual behavior tends to produce estrangement in others which tends to further the unusual behavior. (62)

Phaedrus is presented as a Cassandra figure, silenced by categorical exclusion and his associates' inability to think in his terms. Presenting Phaedrus in this way challenges conventional assumptions about mental aberration as well as salvaging Phaedrus's ideas. It also breaks the silence that enshrouded those ideas.

The issue of silencing is more prominent in Wiesel's work than in any of the others, because the silencings he has encountered have been more extreme. He opens the autobiography by showing how oppression and fear silence in his story of Moche the town beadle. Like Jeremiah, Moche is a prophet, silenced by the refusal of his people to hear his warnings. He returns from captivity to tell a tale of unbelievable atrocities committed upon Jewish deportees, who were driven to the heart of a forest and made to dig their own graves:

> And when they had finished their work, the Gestapo began theirs. Without passion, without haste, they slaughtered their prisoners. Each one had to go up to the hole and present his neck. Babies were thrown into the air and the machine gunners used them as targets. This was in the forest of Galicia near Kolomaye. How had Moche the Beadle escaped? Miraculously. He was wounded in the leg and taken for dead. (4)

No one will believe Moche because they do not want to confront the horror of his story and its implications for themselves. Desperately trying to warn his townspeople of what awaited them, Moche weeps at their disbelief:

> 'You don't understand,' he said in despair. 'You can't understand. I have been saved miraculously. I managed to get back here. Where did I get the strength from? I wanted to come back to tell you the story of my death. . . . I wanted to come back, and to warn you. And see how it is, no one will listen to me. (5)

Wiesel's own fears are expressed in Moche's story. He, too, feels he has come back to tell the story of his own death to warn the living; he fears saying either too much or too little--fears that either way the truth will not be understood.

Each chapter in *Night* speaks of silencing: atrocity silences. Terror silences. Guilt silences. Loss of all that is normative in daily life silences. If the terms in which one has viewed the world begin to seem false, the relationship between language and the truth of experience becomes unreliable. Wiesel tells of experiencing this bewildering disengagement of lanaguage from life when reading the words of the Talmud, the sacred book that was once his source of life: ". . . it is not that I have forgotten the words, I would still know how to translate them, even to comment upon them. But to speak them does not suffice: they must be sung and I no longer know how."[5]

Ten years later as he wrote his autobiography, Wiesel was still struggling against silencing, writing despite those who admonished him to be silent--despite even his own desire to cease the "intolerable wrestle with words and meanings" and recede into silence. T.W. Adorno, who coined the adage, "No poetry after Auschwitz," believed that "the very reconstruction of intolerable reality can somehow contaminate the writer," and concluded that it is better to remain silent.[6] The primary motive of Wiesel's work is not to be defeated by the problem of language, not to succumb to silence. "What torments me most," he claims, "is . . . the silence of the Jews I live among today."[7] But in order not to be silenced, he must find a way of speaking that can overcome corrupt language, falsifying conventions, and sentimentality.

He found his way in a spare, economical, understated style where only those facts are given that are necessary to the story. Taking Hasidic tales as his model, he created in *Night* a highly anecdotal personal history that reads like a series of parables. Hasidic tales approach the truth by indirection. The rabbinical tradition is to answer a question with a story--ideally a story that will make the hearer reevaluate his question. This is how Wiesel broaches the great and tormenting questions the Holocaust raised.

The strength of the autobiography lies in its limited claims. Not pretending to a comprehensive grasp of what happened during the Third Reich or why, the limited perspective of one victim offers a kind of authority and authenticity that is difficult to dismiss. By leaving open questions, offering no explanations, and concluding inconclusively Wiesel forces the reader to raise and confront the large questions alone and without the comfort of authoritative resolution.

Wiesel worked for several years as a journalist before writing *Night* . The reportorial simplicity in the autobiography is another of its strengths. The profound emotional load this work carries is brilliantly counterbalanced by absence of hyperbole, economy of description, and much straight, unelaborated narration; it reads much like a newspaper report in places, with short sentences and paragraphs, stark, strong images, and little extra verbiage. The text is filled, moreover, with silences--gaps on the pages, abrupt stops, conspicuously sparse description. The haunting last sentences of the book illustrate the technique by which the writer reminds the reader again and again of the indescribable and the unspeakable by his refusal to describe. The narrator recalls the moment when, looking into a mirror for the first time since before his long months of imprisonment, he sees his corpse-like countenance: "The look in his eyes, as they stared into mine, has never left me" (109). We must imagine what that look was. Here, as in so many places, Wiesel brings us to the edge of a vision and leaves the moment to imagination and silence.

Each of these autobiographers was conscious of writing in a field of tension between the possibilities and the limitations of language, trying to revise and revalue old stories as they invented ways of telling the parts that don't get told. They were all, as Eliot wrote,

> Trying to learn to use words, and every attempt
> Is a wholly new start, and a different kind of failure
> Because one has only learnt to get the better of words
> For the thing one no longer has to say, or the way in which
> One is no longer disposed to say it. And so each venture
> Is a new beginning, a raid on the inarticulate . . .

Inappropriate Language

Other writers echo Eliot's sentiments about the limitations and erosions of language: Rich writes of her efforts to bring her vision to language, "Even my tools are the wrong ones for what I have to do."[8] Wolf reflects as she writes her autobiography, "We're talking about the fact that there are other kinds of truth . . . And I ask myself why these truths are always recognized so late, and why it's so difficult to discuss them" (379). Explaining how discourse obscures perception, Pirsig reflects, "We take a handful of sand from the endless landscape of awareness and call that handful of sand the world" (69). Agreeing that language is inadequate to describe the extremities they have witnessed" they experience that inadequacy in a variety of ways. Rich defines the problem in terms of the patriarchal bias so deeply imbedded in the language as to exclude certain modes of perception and kinds of description of experience that she identifies as specifically female. Estelle Jelinek identifies a similar, though less extreme, problem in her study of women's autobiography, claiming that the words available to women to describe experience are ill fitting and need translation into new terms:

> As men, . . . women's experiences would be described in heroic or exceptional terms: alienation, initiation, manhood, apotheosis, transformation, guilt, identity crises, and symbolic journeys. As women, their experiences are viewed in more conventional terms: heartbreak, anger, loneliness, motherhood, humility, confusion, and self-abnegation.[9]

The language, she feels, is misfitted to women's needs.

Wolf's observation about "kinds of truth" extends this notion by suggesting that the language tends to exclude all but certain conventional modes of thought or states of consciousness. Syntactical conventions and the limitations of vocabulary delimit experience largely in terms of conscious life; the inner life is so difficult to bring to language precisely because we have not developed an adequate vocabulary for it, even now. This is, of course, an old problem. Mystics have always had to resort to metaphors to express their moments of insight. Psychologists have had either to do the same or to generate their own peculiar terminologies in order to begin to describe and differentiate the inner universe. But their various descriptions rely heavily upon images and analogies that often seem inexact or strained. Pirsig's comment about the tiny area of awareness we have managed to domesticate in language sums up the problem rather well: the expressible is only a small portion of the spectrum of what may be experienced. As there are many kinds of crisis, so also there are many ways in which human experience exceeds or eludes language.

One of the most obvious difficulties modern writers have with the language is the problem of corruption from misuse. George Steiner analyzed in some detail the alarming extent to which the modern world in general and Nazism in particular have poisoned the German language, and by extension other Western languages as well. He observes that as "the community of traditional values is splintered, words themselves have been twisted and cheapened, . . . the classic forms of statement and metaphor are yielding to complex, transitional modes.[10]

We try to compensate for some of this decay by appropriating terms from different theological, political, or psychological systems, but those terms, too, often become slippery and lose their shape through the erosive effect of common usage. They become less and less capable of making us see or feel the realities they name. Langer comments, for instance, on the problem of finding an adequate vocabulary in which to describe the Holocaust: "The problem . . . is to create a language and imagery that will transform mere knowledge into vision and bear the reader beyond the realm of familiar imagining into the bizarre limbo of atrocity."[11] The tendency to reduce or falsify the unfamiliar by assimilating it under familiar rubrics is very strong; we tend to stretch paradigms as far as possible before discarding them and creating new ones.

That falsification is exacerbated by collective retreat from self-confrontation that produces comforting and blinding euphemisms to make social ills tolerable. "We can no longer tell exactly what we have experienced," Wolf writes, and she goes on to explain:

> Today you know that the honest word doesn't exist in the age of suspicion, because the honest speaker depends on an honest listener, and because the person who hears the distorted echo of his own words eventually loses his honesty. (362)

Every set of terms arises from a context of assumptions. The problem in describing crisis, change, or extremity is to free words from conventions, to redeem or renew their meanings, to shape them to the contours of lived experience, and to make readers hear them in a new way. Since language is not simply a means of communication, but also an articulation of shared assumptions, it is difficult for one who does not share those assumptions to communicate what he or she sees. This is particularly true or writers who have to use common language to express uncommon experiences. How do you present the unfamiliar in terms of the familiar? How do you make of language a medium transparent enough to preserve the immediacy of experience?

One way of compensating for the inadequacy of available vocabularies is to redefine them. C.S. Lewis finds that the Christian rhetoric once so natural and familiar to him fails him in his moments of despair. Suddenly not only the pious cliches, but even the complex language of theology seems insufficient, and the renowned Christian apologist becomes virtually inarticulate. Twenty years earlier Lewis had discussed "the problem of pain," exploring pain from a theological standpoint.[12] The terms of that problem come to seem beside the point in the worst throes of grief. He can find no way to speak that is not distorted either by sentimentality or by excessive rationality. In the first pages of his journal he fumbles for words to describe his feelings. He can only describe grief in terms of its surface appearance, not the deeper currents of emotion:

> No one ever told me that grief felt so like fear. I am not afraid, but the sensation is like being afraid. The same fluttering in the stomach, the same restlessness, the yawning. I keep on swallowing. At other times it

> feels like being mildly drunk, or concussed. There is a sort of invisible blanket between the world and me. (1)

Later he takes up the problem of rhetoric directly. He recalls the words of comfort offered him: "She is at peace," "She is with God," "She is in God's hands," and asks himself whether they really have meaning for him now. He realizes that one thing grief has done to him is to shake him out of "merely verbal thinking" and "merely notional beliefs." But the nearer he approaches the "truth" of his experience, the less capable it seems of expression.

By the end of his weeks of writing, Lewis does come to terms with language, but only by acknowledging its inadequacies and by undertaking to infuse old forms with new meaning. By writing about his grief he tries to break down the barrier of incomprehension that surrounds a mourner. His opening phrase, "No one ever told me . . .," recurs in the pages of the journal like a literary watchword as he tries to find a way to tell what he was never told, to render grief communicable. He realizes that complete empathy is impossible. "You can't really share someone else's weakness, or fear or pain," he writes. "What you feel may be bad. It might conceivably be as bad as what the other felt, though I should distrust anyone who claimed that it was. But it would still be quite different. . . . It can't be transferred." (14) Nevertheless in his writing Lewis attempts to bridge the gap that encloses each man in his own suffering.

As writers struggle to find language for such experiences, the nature of language itself frequently becomes a focus of the writing. In *A Sorrow Beyond Dreams* Handke addresses not only the problem of articulating grief, and the inadequacy of language to express it, but the more general problem of language as a surface which must be penetrated to reach interior truths. His own inarticulate grief and his mother's silent despair convince him that language belongs to the "outer world" and that the "inner world" can only be approached indirectly, by metaphor or implication. Language, he concludes, is a camouflage for the lives of quiet desperation that most people lead.

Handke finds, too, that language has a centrifugal quality that pulls one away from the unique, the particular, and the internal. When he feels himself to be most "inside" his mother's character, he finds that no available formulations really communicate the quality of her experience; he finds himself being seduced by the typical and the formulaic in the interests of being understood. At times, he is able fully to identify with his mother, able to experience vicariously the extremity of her feelings. But to speak of those moments requires some compromise with conventional forms of discourse:

> At best, I am able to capture my mother's story for brief moments in dreams, because then her feelings become so palpable that I experience them as doubles and am identical with them; but these are precisely the moments I have already mentioned, in which extreme need to communicate coincides with extreme speechlessness. That is why I affect the usual biographical pattern and write: 'At that time . . . later,' 'Because . . . although,' 'was . . . became . . . became nothing,' hoping in this way to dominate the horror. (31)

The rhetorical formulas of storytelling enable the story to be told and yet conceal as much as they communicate. Caught between speechlessness and the need to speak, between "facts" and "formulations," the author pauses in the middle of his writing to ponder the paradoxical nature of his task:

> I first took the facts as my starting point and looked for ways of formulating them. But I soon noticed that in looking for formulations I was moving away from the facts. I then adopted a new approach--starting not with the facts but with the already available formulations, the linguistic deposit of man's social experience. From my mother's life, I sifted out the elements that were already foreseen in these formulas, for only with the help of a ready-made public language was it possible to single

> out from among all the irrelevant facts of this life the few that cried out to be made public. Accordingly, I compare, sentence by sentence, the stock of formulas applicable to the biography of a woman with my mother's particular life; the actual work of writing follows from the agreements and contradictions between them. (29)

Working inward from the linguistic surface, the writer looks for points of contact between words and moments of being. He finds that the only way to present the truth is dialectically--by holding the spoken and the unspeakable in suspension, calling conventional formulas into question even as he uses them, persistently qualifying, maintaining a precarious balance in a field of tension where every statement has to resist polarization. The writer's dilemma is analogous to the dilemma of the woman he writes about; for both expression is a central problem. Living is expressing, and succumbing to silence a kind of death. That is why Handke wants so urgently not only to feel what his mother felt, but to tell about it. "In stories," he writes,

> we often read that something or other is 'unnameable' or 'indescribable'; ordinarily this strikes me as a cheap excuse. This story, however, is really about the nameless, about speechless moments of terror. It is about moments when the mind boggles with horror, states of fear so brief that speech always comes too late . . . (30).

The text itself is part of that "speech which always comes too late." The restoration it effects is only symbolic. Yet the transformation of his mother's life into story not only endows that life with meaning but also enables the writer to move beyond the deadening paralysis of his own grief.

Through his long meditation upon that life, Handke develops an acute sensitivity to the linguistic biases that enclose women in a world that defines and subordinates them and relegates them to silence. Language is part of the cage in which women like his mother are entrapped until they lose their desire to escape. He begins to recognize the claim that so many feminists have made in the last decades: that language is an instrument of the patriarchy.

That claim resounds through *Of Woman Born*, where Rich, examining the assumptions and expectations superimposed upon the "institution" of motherhood, comes to realize how difficult it is to describe the experience accurately in the terms available. She calls her subject "a ground which seemed to me the most painful, incomprehensible, and ambiguous I had ever travelled, a ground hedged by taboos, mined with false namings" (xvii). To navigate that ground she draws and preserves an essential distinction between the experience of motherhood and the various descriptions of it, looking, as Handke does, for the places where she can recognize points of contact between the formulations and the facts. "Throughout the book," she writes in her introduction,

> I try to distinguish between two meanings of motherhood, one superimposed on the other: the *potential relationship* of any woman to her powers of reproduction and to children; and the *institution* , which aims at ensuring that that potential--and all women--shall remain under male control. . . . This book is not an attack on the family or on mothering, *except as defined and restricted under patriarchy* . (xv, xvi)

The imprisoning effects of male rhetoric are a recurrent theme in the book. For conscious women, she points out, the problem of language is twofold: in the language we share a great deal of female experience remains unnamed because the naming of experience has traditionally been a masculine prerogative; one mode of perception (the public, institutional, masculine) is privileged over the other (the private, contextual, relational, empathetic).[13] These are not simply semantic problems, but obstacles to creative thought and free conduct of life. Rich claims that the problems male judgment has created for the female writer are "problems of contact with herself, problems of language and style, problems of energy and survival." 14 *Of Woman Born* is her effort to define and confront those problems directly: Rich introduces her book as her attempt to reestablish contact with the self that poured into long, anguished journal entries the frustrations, uncertainties, and rage of her young motherhood: "This book," she writes,

> is rooted in my past. . . . Every journey into the past is complicated by delusions, false memories, false namings of real events. I avoided this journey back because it meant going back into pain and anger that I would have preferred to think of as long since resolved and put away. (xvii)

In a chapter entitled "The Sacred Calling" she examines the "problems of language and style" that obscure the experience of motherhood, listing the various euphemisms that have enshrined and rigidified motherhood as an idea:

> Institutionalized motherhood demands of women maternal 'instinct' rather than intelligence. . . . Motherhood is 'sacred' so long as its offspring are 'legitimate'--that is, as long as the child bears the name of a father who legally controls the mother. It is woman's 'highest and holiest mission' . . . (24)

In her autobiography Rich sought to move from the position of defined to definer--from passive acquiescence to active choice--from being a character in an ongoing social drama to becoming an author.

The task began with naming--changing the terms in which she told herself and others her story. Rich describes herself as a "woman sworn to lucidity." Part of that lucidity is achieved by sensitivity to the etymology, usage, and connotative impact of the words we use to describe our lives. She attempts both to expose and to subvert the bias in those words. She perceives her own crisis to have arisen from the damaging effects of falsifying rhetoric; therefore her attempt to heal herself and to help heal the breaches in the community of women centers on finding a just way of speaking.

The problem is, of course, not a new one. In *Testament of Youth* Brittain takes issue with the standard descriptions of war that leave women's contributions and experiences entirely out of account. The "woman question" was integrally connected with Brittain's decision to write and the form she chose. At the time she wrote her autobiography, she had publicly identified herself as both pacifist and feminist. Her desire to demythologize the militaristic ethic and its spurious rhetoric went hand in hand with her concern for what war and its support structures did to women's lives.

Brittain attacked two kinds of rhetoric as blinding and falsifying. One was the language of patriotism, infused with terminology from chivalry and sportsmanship, and the other religious rhetoric that weakened incentives to seek peace and inured the masses to the evils of war. The language that allowed men to glorify war was in large part a cause of what she called "history's grievous repetitions." Believing that if language could so contribute to destruction, it could also heal, she used it as her weapon against war. Brittain recognized what Paul Fussell has called "the simultaneous and reciprocal process by which life feeds materials to literature while literature returns the favor by conferring forms upon life."[15] Fussell claims that language underwent such enormous change during the war that by 1918 it was impossible to use a whole battery of terms without irony. Pre-war rhetoric he claims, was a language "which two generations of readers had been accustomed to associate with the quiet action of personal control and Christian self-abnegation ('sacrifice'), as well as with more violent actions of aggression and defense."[16] This language included Biblical phrases like "fighting the good fight," and "keeping the faith." It also included terminology derived from sports. Journalistic formulas had, he points out, "a familiar, sportsmanlike, Explorer Club overtone, suggesting that what was happening was not too far distant from playing games, running races, and competing in a thoroughly decent way."[17] How to describe war apart from these frames of reference was a problem that increased with prolonged exposure to horror. Everyone at the front who picked up a pen to write a letter home faced this difficulty. The press had one vocabulary for what was happening that non-participants tended to absorb; the participants had another--or none at all. Horror silences. One can describe the scenes that create the horror in vivid, clinical detail, but the horror itself remains nameless. Brittain included, for instance, two excerpts from letters from her fiance--one written before and one after his exposure to trench life. Early in the war he wrote,

> I feel that I am meant to take an active part in this War. It is to me a very fascinating thing--something, if often horrible, yet very ennobling and very beautiful, something whose elemental reality raises it above the reach of all cold theorizing. (103-104)

In a later letter his tone changes markedly:

> Let him who thinks War is a glorious, golden thing, who loves to roll forth stirring words of exhortation, invoking Honour and Praise and Valour and Love of Country . . . let him but look at a little pile of sodden grey rags that cover half a skull and a shinbone and what might have been its ribs, . . . and let him realise how grand and glorious a thing it is to have distilled all Youth and Joy and Life into a foetid heap of hideous putrescence! Who is there who has known and seen who can say that Victory is worth the death of even one of these? (198)

Fussell has brilliantly articulated the problem of patriotic rhetoric in World War I. The way in which it camouflaged atrocity can be seen now as a prelude to the powerful and massively destructive exploitation of rhetoric in World War II. Of the effects of public language in that second war, Sidra Ezrahi writes,

> The soldier-writers of World War II still marched into battle under the cover of what were thought to be invincible literary conventions reflecting the fixed challenges and virtues of combat. They returned under a different banner, bloodied irreparably by a new kind of mechanized and brutal warfare. The violence committed on the meliorist visions of society, as well as on the fortress of the self and the surviving traditions of chivalry, which would begin to find an idiom of its own in the literature of World War II, is carried to an all but inarticulable extreme in the Holocaust.[18]

The problem of language, particularly the German language and its role in the creation of the atrocities of the Third Reich, has been much discussed. Ezrahi claims that "no single language was so transformed by the operation of the Nazi system as was the German language, whose syntax, style, and symbolic associations were profoundly and abidingly violated by what came to be known as 'Nazi-Deutsch,' the perverse rhetoric that signified the collective actions of the National Socialists."[19] George Steiner makes a similar observation in his essay, "The Hollow Miracle," where he writes that the German language was "not only infected with these great bestialities. It was called upon to enforce innumerable falsehoods, to persuade the Germans that the war was just and everywhere victorious."[20] He even goes so far as to claim that German has become useless for ordinary purposes:

> Use a language to conceive, organize, and justify Belsen; use it to make out specifications for gas ovens; use it to dehumanize man during twelve years of calculated bestiality. Something will happen to it. . . . Something of the lies and sadism will settle in the marrow of the language. . . . The language will no longer grow and freshen. It will no longer perform, quite as well as it used to, its two principal functions: the conveyance of humane order which we call law, and

> the communication of the quick of the human spirit which we call grace.[21]

Since World War II the problem of language has reached unprecedented dimensions. Not only words, but conventional forms of discourse and the artistic imagination have been infected in the way Steiner describes. Sidra Ezrahi sees the situation of the post-World War II writer as having reached an outer limit:

> The disjunction between generic memory and conventional forms on the one hand, and 'millenial' subject matter and the literary forms which have evolved to contain the new reality on the other, is a measure of the shifts in the boundaries of art beyond which the imagination becomes inarticulate and form disintegrates altogether.[22]

The renewal of language in the aftermath of corruptions and distortions of this magnitude is a work of imagination that must begin at the most fundamental level: pulling back the euphemistic veils, being willing actively to pursue "the thing itself and not the myth," and naming what we see.

Naming

"The first thing they tried to destroy was the names," Wiesel recalled in an interview about his months in Auschwitz.

> When they reduced man to a number, they took away his name. When they reduced him to an object they took away his name. An inmate in the camp was not allowed to keep his name. . . I think nothing can be more denigrating, nothing can be more humiliating than to take a name away.[23]

According to the Genesis myth, the power of naming was the first power given to man. Because naming and names have such deeply rooted religious, psychological, and practical significance, the denial of that power is a particularly oppressive form of silencing. Naming oneself is one of the primary acts of freedom--an imitation, some would say, of the divine "I AM." One of the first memories Wolf records in *A Model Childhood* is sitting, as a very small child, on the doorstep of her father's store, "trying the new word out in her mind: I . . . I . . . I . . . I . . . I . . . each time with a thrilled shock which had to be kept a secret. . ." (5).

Naming is a power not only in a religious sense, but in the social and political realm as well. To name something is to validate its existence and to determine its mode of being by breaking through the obliterating silence of anonymity. In a very real sense we are in the power of those who give us names. Mary Daly, the feminist theologian, sees the denial of the power of naming to women as one of the fundamental injustices of patriarchy. "Women," she claims, "have had the power of naming stolen from us" But she goes on to point out that in recent years women are "beginning to come to grips with the problem of our own self-naming in a world in which women are nameless.

Naming takes place on multiple levels, beginning with the names by which the author chooses to designate himself on the cover of his book, and in the text. It is significant, for example, that Brittain retained her maiden name for the purpose of authorship and in fact never names her husband in her books except by an initial: G. Brittain was aware of the ways in which the institution of marriage "[took] away a woman's individuality" (642). After a war which she had survived only by a long, gradual, painful eroding of personality, recovery began with reassertion of her individuality. Retaining her birth name was a refusal to "give herself up" by giving her name away.

Wiesel's name was important to him for different reasons. He, too, made a point of reclaiming his name, which was "taken from him" when the SS engraved a number on his arm. It was the last link remaining with the native tradition that gave his life historical context and meaning. In an interview Wiesel explained,

> The return of names, the eternity of names, and the destiny of names has always fascinated me. Therefore, I'm very careful with names. I choose names prudently; they always have a certain meaning, a special meaning to me.[24]

To a people so often homeless and without a nation, names have been more importantly than to most a sign of connection with the community that gives them identity and a reminder of their legacy as a "chosen people." Wiesel's naming of himself in *Night* is both a reaffirmation and a new use of that tradition; he is no longer able, after Auschwitz, to identify with it in the same way; the reaffirmation of Judaism in much of his writing is at the same time a radical reinterpretation of the meaning of that tradition.

Wolf describes how the fictitious name for her childhood self "came to her" as she began to write her autobiography:

> At this point the mother would have to call the child in for supper, from the living-room window. For the first time we hear the name by which the child will be called in these pages: Nelly! (And thus, quite incidentally, the baptismal formalities have been taken care of, without dwelling on the tedious search for a suitable name.) (6)

This highly self-conscious splitting of the self is an effort, she explains, to break the "hegemony" of the past "which can still split the first person into the second and the third" (406). The aim of telling her story in this way is to reunite the parts of herself that she has separated; the separation is an imitation of what the circumstances of her life have done to her sense of herself, the reunification is her act of healing. "The final point," she writes, "would be reached when the second and the third person were to meet again in the first, or, better still, were to meet with the first person. When it would no longer have to be 'you' and 'she' but a candid, unreserved 'I'" (349). Wolf fuses facts and fictions of the self, naming both herself and her experience in a new way, breaking the silences and taboos that have surrounded her throughout her adult life with an aura of guilt. She claims her own self-styled identity and disclaims the parts of an old identity she is no longer willing to validate. Like all autobiographies, hers is an answer to the primary question, "Who am I?"

Adrienne Rich addresses that question in an equally self-conscious way. For women, she believes, self-naming means overcoming deeply implanted cultural messages that teach women to distrust their own perceptions. She observes, "patriarchy calls something by a pejorative name and you start thinking of it as a negative value. It may be a positive strength to you but it's always been named pejoratively" (114).

"Writing is re-naming," Rich declares in her essay, "When We Dead Awaken." Both in that autobiographical essay and in *Of Woman Born* she explores the effects of "that female fatigue of suppressed anger and the loss of contact with her own being." She claims that the motive of her writing, and of much women's writing in our time, is a "drive to self-knowledge" which for a woman is "more than a search for identity: it is part of her refusal of the self-destructiveness of male-dominated society."[25] Writing is thus a "difficult and dangerous walking on the ice, as we try to find language and images for a consciousness we are just coming to," an attempt to change unexamined concepts of sexual identity, and to name oneself in some way that does not label and subordinate.(91)

Peter Handke signifies his awareness of and sympathy with this "nameless" condition of women in his narration of his mother's life story by pointedly leaving her nameless. The story of her life is a chronicle of depersonalization and diminishment that ends in self-destruction. He presents her case as, paradoxically, both extreme and typical--a logical consequence of a common condition: obliteration by anonymity.

C.S. Lewis attests to the significance of names in a different way. He chooses not to call his wife by her name in the text of his journal, but designates her by an initial--"H." His concern for preserving the privacy of names is further reflected in his decision to use a pseudonym. *A Grief Observed* was the only one of his many works to which he did not sign his own name, not only for the sake of privacy, but also out of sensitivity to the possibility that the book might give scandal to those who knew and revered him as a Christian apologist and a model of strong faith. The pseudonym, "N.W. Clerk," is a play on the Anglo-Saxon for "I know not what scholar." It is therefore a name that proclaims a right to anonymity--an interesting contrast to the necessity women writers like Brittain and Daly and Rich feel to make their names their own by making them public.

The term "naming" is broad, including more than actual self-designation; it extends to the naming of experience--the generating of a descriptive vocabulary that includes suppressed areas of experience. When naming becomes labelling, it is a destructive and oppressive act. Labels fail to differentiate. Their object is not to identify, but to obscure identity. Reflecting on the uses of the term "Jew" in wartime Germany, George Steiner observed that it was used without any reference to the differences among Jews: "The anti-Semite is no theologian; but his definition is inclusive. So we would all have gone together, the Orthodox and I. And the gold teeth would have come out of our dead mouths, song or no song."[26]

The naming of experience and the naming of the self in these autobiographies is thus a reclaiming of a fundamental right for persons coming out of a situation of powerlessness, oppression, or loss of self. As an exercise of power it both signifies and enacts the return of authority in an act that is sometimes violent, sometimes defiant, and often triumphant with relief like the cry of Sylvia Plath's Esther Greenwood as she runs from the scene of a suicide that might have been her own: "I am! I am! I am!"[27]

Appropriating Language

At some point, everyone who puts pen to paper experiences the frustrating difficulty of finding words to correspond to idea or experience. This problem is magnified enormously when the writer is attempting to express an extreme experience or an idea that is radically unconventional. In 1921 Edward Sapir wrote,

> The birth of a new concept is invariably foreshadowed by a more or less extended use of old linguistic material; the concept does not attain to individual and independent life until it has found a distinctive linguistic embodiment. . . . As soon as the word is at hand, we instinctively feel, with something of a sigh of relief, that the concept is ours for the handling. Not until we own the symbol do we feel that we hold a key to the immediate knowledge or understanding of the concept.[28]

Every writer is called upon to strike some compromise with language in his efforts to turn it to his own purposes, and in the process to reform language in some way.

The problem of finding words for inexpressible things exists in varying degrees, and has been posed in different terms depending upon the nature of the experiences the writer seeks to express. Handke poses it in terms of the discrepancy between the inner and the outer world--between surface and interior, and works with language as a surface or mask. The effort to use language to reveal or articulate the inner life always results in a paradox. Words must be used and subverted at the same time.

Feminist writers have addressed the problem in more specific objections to the way Western languages describe general human experience in categories that leave out whole areas of experience--often female experience. Language tends to make maleness normative.[29] In a language that so frequently equates or connects femininity with the negative, women find it difficult to tell their stories in positive terms or convey the seriousness or importance of female experience. After listening to a large group of women tell their personal stories, Carol Gilligan observed,

> The difficulty women experience in finding or speaking publicly in their own voices emerges repeatedly in the form of qualification and self-doubt, but also in intimations of a divided judgment, a public assessment and private assessment which are fundamentally at odds.[30]

Like all writers in a state of transition or crisis, women writers face the task of appropriating a language ill fitted to what they want to say and tailoring it to their needs.

Crisis narratives offer particularly graphic examples of strategies adopted to reappropriate and recycle language. If struggle with language is a part of every crisis, coming to terms with language is an essential part of healing--of regaining inner integrity and reuniting oneself with the larger world. One of these strategies is direct attack: at some point in their narratives, every one of the writers examined here discusses the problem of language, qualifying their use of words, challenging the reader to question conventional usage, and liberating themselves to redefine the terms of common discourse.

One aspect of this strategy is to show how particular words have become labels, to point out the value-load certain words carry and their consequent indoctrinating effect, to "unmask" words. In both Handke's and Rich's writing the mask-like quality of language becomes a dominant theme. This archaeological examination of words and meanings is a process of making language strange--heightening awareness of words by using them in a slightly unorthodox way. This kind of defamiliarization is a way of making people see, for, as Pirsig observes, "What makes [Phaedrus's] world so hard to see clearly is not its strangeness but its usualness. Familiarity can blind you too" (63). Wolf makes examination and redefinition of common words a motif in her work. Numerous passages in *A Model Childhood* elaborate the implications and associations contained in a single word. Thus she begins her fourteenth chapter:

> *Verfallen*--a German word. A look into foreign language dictionaries: nowhere else these four, five different meanings. German youth is addicted--*verfallen*--to its Fuehrer. The bill drawn on the future is forfeited--verfallen. Their roofs are dilapidated--verfallen. But you must have known that she's a wreck--*verfallen*. No other language knows *verfallen* in the sense of 'irretrievably lost,' because enslaved by one's own, deep-down consent. (288)

With each repetition the word becomes more suggestive, and the formative power of language more obvious as examination of language becomes examination of experience. As in Handke's book, language is revealed here as a surface to be penetrated--not by pushing past it to "meaning" in some abstract sense, but by attending minutely to the singular lives of the words themselves.

Each of these writers chooses certain key words that become a nexus of thought--words whose definition, like Wolf's *verfallen* proceeds from and determines a world view--words that abound with associations, generating both memories and speculations.

For Pirsig one of these words is "Quality." Much of his exploration of his own intellectual history as well as his speculations about Western society rests upon the definition of that term. He defines "caring" and "Quality" as the missing elements in Western technological values, and concludes,

> if care and Quality are external and internal aspects of the same thing, then it follows logically that what really causes technological hopelessness is absence of the perception of Quality in technology by both technologists and anti-technologists. Phaedrus' mad pursuit of the rational, analytic and therefore *technological* meaning of the word "Quality" was really a pursuit of the answer to the whole problem of

> technological hopelessness. . . . to understand the meaning of Quality in classic terms required a backup into metaphysics and its relationship to everyday life--namely, formal reason. . . . Quality is the Buddha. Quality is scientific reality. Quality is the goal of Art. It remains to work these concepts into a practical, down-to-earth context, and for this there is nothing more practical or down-to-earth than what I have been talking about--the repair of an old motorcycle. (247-48)

The ensuing discussion and personal narrative are thus introduced as context for understanding this key term--an ordinary word defined in an extraordinary way instills a new consciousness of its implications for ordinary life. Redefinition and elaboration are the two essential elements in Pirsig's narrative strategy. Ordinary words become doors into long, branching corridors of thought.

Another strategy is either partial or wholesale rejection of certain languages or linguistic categories. Many Jews who survived the Holocaust, for instance, have, like Wiesel, opted to give up their native tongue because it is too resonant with the brutalities they suffered to be usable to them. Wiesel explained in an interview, "Had I wanted to write in Hungarian, I would have had an easier task, but I didn't want to. I even tried to forget Hungarian. The Hungarian language reminded me too much of the Hungarian gendarmes and they were brutal."[31] Wiesel adopted French and has written most of his popular works in French since the 1950's. The French language, he says, "became a haven, a new beginning, a new possibility, a new world. To start expressing myself in a new language was a defiance."[32] For similar reasons a number of post-war writers adopted English rather than their native languages, reasoning, as Ezrahi explains it, that

> in its very remoteness from the events, [English] retains a kind of autonomy and purity that only a language which was not spoken in the concentrationary universe,

> and was therefore never tainted by the Holocaust vocabulary, could claim. . . . English represented not only the 'sound of defiance,' but also the very existence of another world and a different hierarchy of values.[33]

Another way of revitalizing language is to use words sparingly. Deliberate omission of certain words or figures of speech creates conspicuous pockets of silence. The post-Holocaust writer Piotr Rawicz declared his intention to "ban 'figures of speech' altogether, to 'kill comparisons,' and to 'engage in mere recounting, mere enumeration,"[34] thus stripping language down to the bare bones in an effort to purify it--an extreme method, suited to extreme circumstances.

In a slightly different way, Wiesel also adopted a strategy of distillation and reduction to essentials in *Night*, a series of stark, sparsely described vignettes built upon vivid centralizing images economically elaborated. "Nothing but the substance must be said," he declared--"Nothing but the essential. We have no more time, no more patience to play around with words."[35] In his view, language emerges from and returns to a great silence, and the writer who lives on the edge of that silnce must build a bridge between the spoken and the unspeakable, as simply and elegantly as an architect who wastes not a single piece of his material. When asked whether he thought the prostitution of words an "artistic sin," Wiesel replied emphatically that the misuse of words is "a sin, period! Words are no longer innocent; words are dangerous. . . . The first sin is a sin against language. I think man begins to sin by prostituting language. The writer who does this prostitutes himself."[36] An event like the Holocaust makes it hard to overestimate the power of rhetoric to change the world. Wiesel tries to counter that vast, still echoing outpouring of destructive rhetoric with writing that constantly reiterates the value of silence.

A less extreme approach to the problem of language is the dialectical technique exemplified in Handke's narrative. He deliberately creates fields of tension between experience and language, between language and silence, between one set of terms and another, between one level of diction and another. The effect of such juxtapositions is most often ironic. Brittain's method of exposing and disarming the biases of public discourse is another example of this kind of dialectic. She juxtaposes public and private modes of expression--the language of patriotism and the language of visceral experience--conventional and idiosyncratic formulations.

Wolf and Rich throw public language into question by making private modes of speech public, thus creating a tension between two radically different descriptions of experience. When Rich opposes "institution" to "experience," she establishes the poles of her own discourse and a fundamental distinction between two linguistic modes, just as Wolf opposes public, institutionalized descriptions of wartime Germany to her own memories.

Another means of appropriating and reclaiming language is by translation or analogy: the use of an established terminology in a context that changes its meaning. Brittain, for instance, uses the language of the Christian tradition she has rejected to express a very secular view of her survival:

> The fact that, within ten years, I lost one world, and after a time rose again, as it were, from spiritual death to find another, seems to me one of the strongest arguments against suicide that life can provide. There may be--I believe there is not--resurrection after death, but nothing could prove more conclusively than my own brief but eventful history the fact that resurrection is possible within our limited span of earthly time. (410)

Her use of the Christian paradigm has two effects: it makes her ideas accessible by analogy, but at the same time ironizes the rhetorical paradigm itself.

Wiesel's use of the language of Jewish theology is similar to Brittain's appropriation of Christian rhetoric, but more complex and extensive. Though no longer a believing Jew in the same sense as before the war,

Wiesel finds the vocabulary of Jewish experience most suited to expressing his profound disillusionment. His intent in using religious terminology is not, like Brittain's, to ironize it as seriously and radically to reinterpret it.

A much-debated example of this kind of personalization of standardized rhetoric is Sylvia Plath's use of the language and imagery of Nazism and the Holocaust to describe the "inner hell" she inhabited in her periods of mental illness. Irving Howe strenuously objected to Plath's appropriation of that vocabulary of experience:

> The images of her skin as a Nazi lampshade, of ashes, a cake of soap, a gold filling to invoke vision of her own death . . . the fantasy of her German-born father as a Nazi and herself as a Jewish victim, meant to represent the problematic father-daughter relationship; the kitchen oven emblematic of the crematory ovens and the fat of the Sunday lamb recalling the fat of the Jews. . . are manifestations of the process by which Sylvia Plath came to regard herself as 'an imaginary Jew from the concentration camps of the mind.'[37]

All of these applications he found overwrought and egotistically inappropriate. Ezrahi, too, finds Plath's personal appropriation of that language offensive. She observes that "when the vocabulary of the events of 1933-45 is applied to any situation of intense emotional or social privation, the enormity and the moral inadmissability of the concentrationary experience are diluted even as the widespread symbolic assimilation of the experience is achieved."[38] Undeniably, however, Plath's creation of such an analogy conveys a powerful sense of the quality of emotional and mental torment she attempts to describe.

All of these methods are ways of reclaiming language from erosion and corruption and of compensating for its limitations. Never are those limitations so apparent as when a person in extremity attempts to describe it. Since he cannot easily separate the tale from the telling, the difficulties of telling become part of the tale. All of these writers were engaged in a searching, often agonizing process of claiming and personalizing language in their efforts to tell something that must, yet cannot be told. As Wiesel put it,

> When we write, we write with words and these words come from somewhere. These words have already been said and uttered thousands and millions of times. And then there is some mystery that takes place when I take these words and make them mine.[39]

If language is their burden, it is also the source of their regeneration.

Appropriating Silence

In a recent interview, Wiesel reiterated a belief that justifies and explains the motive of his writing: that words lead us toward silence, that the expressible, if it is true, tends always in the direction of the inexpressible. "If I could communicate a Silence through silence," he said, "I would do so. But I cannot. Perhaps I am not strong enough or wise enough. I try to communicate that Silence with words.[40]

Wiesel's consciousness of language is extraordinarily acute because he believes it is his vocation to write about an experience many believe to be "beyond description." Since 1945 his efforts to find ways to "purify" and renew language, and to use words to make readers aware of the mysteries that do lie beyond language have resulted in a sparse, stark style, always afraid of saying too much. Of many modern writers he says,"most of them talk too much. Their song is lost in words, like rivers in the sand."[41] Wiesel's own words resonate in their simplicity, ending in paradox illuminating the silence that lies at the heart of them. Like Eliot, Wiesel believes that "words, after speech, reach into the silence." It is that silence that needs to be heard.

Despite his misgivings about modern verbosity, Wiesel's sense of the overwhelming, challenging presence of Silence as antagonist and partner in an ongoing dialogue is something he shares with many modern writers. Ihab Hassan claims that in the twentieth century, "Literature has adopted a new attitude toward itself, and silence is its metaphor."42 Modern literature "aspires to silence," in the same manner that Pater claimed that all art aspires to the condition of music. Reaching toward the inexpressible, he reminds us, characterized the Romantic enterprise. One recent critic has characterized Romanticism by "all those Romantic adjectives indicating a mysterious area of human experience outside logic and conventional attitudes . . . 'abominable,' 'interminable,' 'unfathomable,' or 'impenetrable." Hassan claims that what we are seeing now is the "nocturnal side" of that romantic impulse. The silences in modern literature are more sinister than ecstatic or mystical.

What Hassan observes about literature in general is certainly true of modern autobiography, a genre increasingly focused upon kinds of experience that have driven men and women into silence. Insofar as autobiography focuses upon the marginal or the extreme, it has to come to terms with the limits of the expressible, to push language to its limits and extend those limits.

Silence has therefore become an essential part of the writer's vocabulary. Conscious of what language cannot do, they attempt to find new ways to appropriate and stretch the limits of language, and to appropriate silence as well. The range of the expressible, like the range of the visible or audible, covers only a partial spectrum of experience. They seek to make their texts instruments which increase that range like the lenses that extend our capacities to see beyond what offers itself to the naked eye.

George Steiner claims that since World War II artists have been in "retreat from the word." Those who live by words use them with unprecedented self-consciousness, caution, and qualification. They do, however, continue to use them, prolifically. What has also changed is their use of silence. Silence has assumed an increasingly prominent role as theme and metaphor in modern writing. As silence has become more thematic, its role in narration has become more differentiated. It functions as urtext, as context, as subtext, as antagonist, as protagonist, as theme, as telos. The encounter with silence seems to be an essential part of bringing experience to language. Wiesel goes so far as to identify the poetic vocation with this encounter. "In general," he says, "you can recognize a poet by the way he speaks of silence. I think that every poet, at one time or another, must come to speak about silence."43 Silence is the starting place for every writer as well as the end toward which writing proceeds--the alpha and omega of language.

Silence is also a generative force. Each of these autobiographical narratives arises out of an experience of silencing, proceeds out of that silence and is shaped by it, as by a center of gravity. The silence each writer has experienced pulls like a black hole; the narrative is a strategy to stay on its outer edge--a struggle for survival and a resistance to the obliteration of memory and the dulling of consciousness.

The idea of resistance rightly implies a kind of violence. Each beginning is a breaking through--a refusal to remain imprisoned and isolated in silence. Each writer is breaking taboos that surround him or her like a wall of silence created by social and literary conventions that circumscribe and dictate what can and ought to be said. Each writer is a Job figure, presuming to enter into dialogue with the great Unknown.

Christa Wolf writes, "What is past is not dead. It is not even past. We cut ourselves off from it; we pretend to be strangers" (3). The past she speaks about is one many would like to bury--particularly her German audience, and most particularly herself. Her writing is an act of courageous resistance to the false comforts derived from suppressing what we find intolerable to contemplate. She will not allow her past to recede into silence, but sets out to explore it on the premise that, as the maxim goes, "if way to the better there be, it exacts a full look at the worst." These encounters with silence are battles for life. Silence is a death force. The writer cannot overcome it, but can shape and control it and bring it into contrapuntal relationship to their words. They can keep it at bay. They can even make it speak.

This struggle with silence is a drama enacted in each narrative. These autobiographers write against silences--of fear or anguish, or pain--which threaten to overwhelm them. Silence is an ocean in which they may drown. Rich's image of the diver images the writer as a descending into an element where her "shabby equipment" offers minimal protection against the pressure which increases the deeper she goes into the unfamiliar medium where language may be obliterated. The writer/diver is subjecting language to extraordinary pressure, and must learn, as she descends, "to move in a different medium." That movement is only partly a matter of control. It is just as much a matter of submission.

Words are, as Hassan puts it, the writer's act of "metaphysical revolt," but also of "metaphysical surrender." Wolf ends her long narrative upon a note of surrender: "I shall not revolt against the limits of the expressible." Thus she appropriately concludes an autobiography that stretches the limits of the expressible further than most. She consents, finally, to keep dream and reality, speech and silence, separate. Ultimately they cannot be fused. Speaking is her revolt. Conceding the limits of language is her surrender.

Silence becomes an overarching metaphor for the absolutes these writers grapple with: despair, suffering, madness, death. They have all approached the outer edge of human experience in either mental or physical suffering, and return not only to tell the tale, but by telling it to push that boundary out a little further. They accomplish that reclamation in various ways. One is paradox. Silence is the vanishing point of paradox. Like a koan, a paradox brings one to a vision which can neither be refuted nor rejected, but must simply be contemplated. Another technique is radical irony. Like paradox, irony silences. Another is to leave gaps in the text--to make the text a network of words woven around silences. Another is suggestiveness, nuance, implication--opening doors and staying at the threshold.

Ultimately the whole undertaking of translating life into text and silence into speech is paradoxical. The reader is led into silence by a narrator who assumes the role of guide, like Virgil, in the infernal and shadowy regions of human experience, but who can only describe it indirectly and incompletely. He can only tell the truth by "telling it slant," and leading the reader to the edges of silence to stand there with him, contemplating the unspoken. Silence is the answer to questions that have no answer.

---

1 Carolyn Heilbrun, introduction to Vera Brittain's *Testament of Experience* (London: Virago Ltd., 1981), p. 2.

2 Adrienne Rich, "When We Dead Awaken" in Gelpi, p. 98.

3 Adrienne Rich, "Three Conversations" in Gelpi, p. 114.

4 Adrienne Rich, "The Phenomenology of Anger" in Gelpi, p. 72.

5 Elie Wiesel, *Legends*, p. 30.

6 Cited in Ezrahi, p. 6.

7 Cargas, p. 8.

8 Adrienne Rich, "The Roofwalkers" in Gelpi, p. 20.

9 Estelle Jelinek, *Women's Autobiography* (Bloomington: Indiana University Press, 1980), introduction.

10 George Steiner, *Language and Silence* (New York: Athenaeum, 1982), p. 11.

11 Lawrence Langer, *Versions of Survival: The Holocaust and the Human Spirit* (Albany: State University of New York Press, 1982), p. 12.

12 C.S. Lewis, *The Problem of Pain* (New York: Macmillan, 1965).

13 Carol Gilligan, *In a Different Voice* (Cambridge, MA: Harvard University Press, 1981), pp. 24 ff.

14 Adrienne Rich, "When We Dead Awaken" in Gelpi, p. 92.

15 Paul Fussell, *The Great War and Modern Memory* (New York: Oxford University Press, 1971), p. ix.

16 Fussell, p. 21.

17 Fussell, p. 21.

18 Ezrahi, p. 3.

[19] Ezrahi, p. 11.

[20] Steiner, p. 100.

[21] Steiner, p. 101.

[22] Ezrahi, p. 3

[23] Cargas, p. 51.

[24] Cargas, p. 50.

[25] Rich, "When We Dead Awaken," in Gelpi, p. 91.

[26] Steiner, p. 142.

[27] Sylvia Plath, *The Bell Jar* (New York: Bantam Books, 1971), p. 115.

[28] Quoted in Casey Miller and Kate Swift, *Words and Women* (New York: Doubleday, Anchor Books, 1977), p. 128.

[29] See for example Gilligan's and Miller and Swift's arguments.

[30] Gilligan, p. 16.

[31] Cargas, p. 65.

[32] Cargas, pp. 665-66.

[33] Ezrahi, p. 12.

[34] Miller and Swift, p. xii.

[35] Ezrahi, p. 55.

[36] Cargas, p. 92.

[37] Cargas, p. 85.

[38] Irving Howe, Letter to the Editor, *Commentary*, October, 1974, p. 12.

[39] Ezrahi, p. 215.

[40] Cargas, p. 112.

[41] Cargas, p. 5.

[42] Ihab Hassan, *The Literature of Silence* (New York: Alfred A. Knopf, 1967), p. xi.

[43] Cargas, p. 49.

CHAPTER 4

QUESTIONS AND ANSWERS

Overwhelming Questions

"The Love Song of J. Alfred Prufrock" opens with an invitation to follow the speaker down "Streets that follow like a tedious argument / of insidious intent / To lead us to an overwhelming question ...." But the question is never asked; the speaker draws back: "Oh, do not ask, What is it?"' Like Prufrock, most of us manage to avoid overwhelming questions most of the time, simply by refusing to ask them. "Behind our own backs," Christa Wolf writes, "we can instruct our memories: Avoid certain memories . . . Suppress words, sentences, whole chains of thought that might give rise to remembering. Don't ask . . . certain questions" (229-30).

Epistemology begins with the basic questions, "What can I know?" and "What must I do?" Autobiographies begin with similar questions. When critic Richard Church says that autobiography is an answer to the question, "Is life worth living?" he is reading autobiography as response, or solution, to a profound question.[1] Kenneth Burke, too, believes that "Critical and imaginative works are answers to questions posed by the situation in which they arose."[2] One way of characterizing an author's work is in terms of the central questions he addresses. H.J. Cargas says of Wiesel's work, for instance: Wiesel resubmits the everlasting question: Who is God? Who am I? What is my relationship to God? What is my relationship to man? All of these questions are implicit in his fiction, but some more specifically than others.[3]

The questions that generate autobiography are never merely academic. They are often, like Prufrock's, overwhelming--threatening questions that one avoids as long as possible. They demand that a person reexamine his or her assumptions, restructure his or her consciousness and possibly change his or her life. They preclude merely intellectual response. They "bring the moment to its crisis. Once they are asked, a Rubicon is crossed, and they must be answered. Robert Lloyd calls the questions that do this the "real" questions--those that affect the whole man, arresting him suddenly in the midst of life and demanding his total attention:

> A real question is not just a thought, or a collection of words or symbols somewhere, or some form of logical structure. A real question is a state of your being, a total state, in which there is suddenly created a large space between thought and action, an empty space across which there are no roads, no tracks, no signposts, no evidence of habitation; you do not know how to start across, what will happen on the other side--if there is one--or why you should undertake the journey.4

In her introduction to *Of Woman Born*, Rich explains how long she avoided coming come to terms with the questions introduced in that book. "For a long time," she writes, "I avoided this journey back . . . because it meant going back into pain and anger that I would have preferred to think of as long since resolved and put away" (xvii). Once the decision was made to take that journey and ask those questions, she was drawn like the diver in her poem into the depths of her own emotional life and into a far-reaching examination of personal and collective history that changed not only her way of thinking, but her way of life.

There is no return, she finds, to pre-crisis assumptions or "innocence." Crisis, like the fall, destroys original integrity and makes change inevitable. To attempt to "go back," to regain what has been lost and restore it as it was before, would be to deny growth and ultimately to deny life. The result would be a diminishment and a disastrous crippling of the soul. Crisis demands creative response. Finding and formulating useful questions and answering them is the beginning of re-creation. Real questions are hard to compose, and take courage to ask; the psychic cost of asking them may be enormous. But the cost may be even greater if they are left unasked. For the sake of sanity, a person in crisis must try to develop a new way of grasping what is real when his or her basic assumptions about the world have been shaken. In such a situation, autobiography becomes a vehicle for asking and answering fundamental questions.

Questions define the zone of inquiry that gives a book its shape. In each of the autobiographies examined here, those core questions are posed quite explicitly. In each case the writing is presented as a quest for answers to questions that break taboos, penetrate forbidden territories, name hidden things, and challenge basic beliefs.

The guiding question in *Of Woman Born*--"What was it like for women?"-- opens a wide field of speculative inquiry whose implications for the author's private and public life are enormously consequential. In this book, Rich examines history from a non-traditional perspective, taking into account women's life stories, measuring the distance between those stories, sociologies, and histories written by men. She begins with her own story, taken from journals she wrote as a young mother in a time of acute stress--a time when her myths and realities were so far apart that she felt torn asunder trying to bridge the chasm between the two. The question she raises, as she reads those journal entries, challenges her to break through old blindnesses and see something new: what were my unexamined assumptions?

In *Testament of Youth* Brittain similarly attempts, by posing unconventional questions, to free a large area of human experience from the orthodox modes of thinking that resist analysis. The book addresses the question, what is war like for the individuals involved in it--and, more specifically, for women. "I might have had children," she reflects, "who would certainly never ask me: 'Mother, what did you do in the Great War?' (651) So she poses the question herself, because it needs asking. Her own story is one answer to the general question that she asks, like Rich: what was it like for women? By particularizing history, she arrives at a set of general truths that challenge prevailing cultural orthodoxy.

Wolf deals with a similarly shattering personal encounter with history, but her questions are more psychological than social. Where Brittain examines the individual life in terms of social and political forces, Wolf examines social and political life in terms of individual psychology. She asks, "How did we become what we are?"--a question that demands an examination of motive and responsibility, of the relationship between the individual conscience and collective action, and which leads her both to indictment of her own past and acceptance of it.

Like Wolf, Pirsig begins his journey into the past with a combination of guilt, ambivalence, and philosophical curiosity. He raises questions about his own inner history that reflect larger questions about the culture of his time. The poles of his own dividedness become a measure of the polarities that have caused cultural schizophrenia on a scale almost too large to be recognized. He begins with haunting questions about his own history: what drove Phaedrus mad? What was the vision he could not sustain among other people? What is valuable about that vision? and most pertinently for the author, what is left of him in me? Who is Phaedrus in relation to who I am now? The last is of course most threatening. To reidentify with the part of himself that went insane is as frightening as Wolf's attempt to reconnect with the part of herself that blindly participated in Nazism. Pirsig writes of himself, "I tend to become taken with philosophic questions, going over them and over them and over them again in loops that go round and round until they either produce an answer or become so repetitively locked on they become psychiatrically dangerous . . ." (14) Questions drove him insane, but questions are also a means of reaffirming his sanity. In the autobiography he rephrases and reconfronts the questions that Phaedrus struggled with and succumbed to, taking on an old challenge to test his strength and sanity.

For Lewis and Wiesel the overwhelming questions are essentially religious. Both cast themselves as latter-day Jobs, crying out for an explanation of suffering, some understanding of it that will make it tolerable. Both deeply religious men, their questions are infused with rending doubts that produce not despair but a resounding "de profundis"--the outcry of a faith strained to its limit. Such originating questions raise others. Every authentic answer contains the seed of a new question. "Answers," Wiesel believes, "only intensify the question."[5]

As questions open new territories of the mind, answering is an effort to stretch and grow to fill those spaces. A question introduces a variety of options: answers can take many forms. The task of the questioner is less to elicit a right answer than to find the "right questions." The "right questions" heal because they appeal to the whole person; to form an answer one must integrate the parts of him- or herself that have been fragmented and bring them together in the frame of reference established by the question. Healing depends, however, on finding the "right questions."

Finding the Right Questions

Job's moment of enlightenment came when he realized he had been asking God the wrong questions. Wrong questions wrongly define the terms of a problem. Right questions reframe a dilemma in terms that allow it to be seen from a more complete perspective. They produce insight, prohibit self-deception, clarify values, expose and articulate assumptions, and generate more questions. They demand confrontation and decision. They make one see what could not be seen before. Right questions are instruments of growth and change; wrong questions are really nonquestions--they challenge nothing. They reinforce preexisting ideas and invite affirmation rather than discussion. They lead to deeper entrenchment in prejudice; they demand only that biases be reaffirmed, dissatisfactions vindicated. They are self-protective. The right questions are always risky; they free a person from the catechetical thinking that produces dogmatic answers, and help him to find language to express what he is experiencing.

Most questions only allow a narrow range of answers. A good question allows a broad range of possibilities. Carol Gilligan reports that in her work with women who were answering psychological questionnaires, many complained that they couldn't answer the questions asked of them, not because they were not clear, but because they were the wrong questions, framed inappropriately to the kinds of experience and reasoning processes the women were attempting to communicate. Answering the questions in the terms posed, they felt, resulted in distortion.6

In "intensive journal" therapy Ira Progoff encourages patients to frame questions as a means of increasing awareness. Thought does not begin with statements, he claims, but with questions. Good questions are endlessly generative and lead to surprises. They are catalysts, suggesting new ways of organizing or connecting different aspects of experience. Thus he asks patients to write out inner dialogues in the form of questions and answers.

Autobiographies are products of such an inner dialogue. An autobiography is always a confrontation: of past self with present self, of one's own voice with the voices of others, of the intellect with the emotions, of general truth with particular truths, of belief with experience. Autobiographies such as those examined here can be read schematically as chains of questions branching outward from the "overwhelming questions" with which they begin. Reading autobiographical texts in terms of these questions reveals several discrete stages in the questioning process.

At first, in the moment of crisis, questioning may simply be a rhetorical gesture, like the desperate outcry of the Psalmist: "Oh, Lord, how long...?" We see this kind of question in *A Grief Observed*, where Lewis cries out in the throes of grief, "Oh God, God, why did you take such trouble to force this creature out of its shell if it is now doomed to crawl back--to be sucked back--into it?" (20) A certain detachment is required to ask questions that are more than cathartic outbursts--that generate creative responses. At one point Lewis deliberately stops himself from making such a rhetorical gesture. Instead, he rephrases it as a question capable of further reflection: "[That] was a yell rather than a thought. Let me try it over again. Is it rational to believe in a bad God? Anyway, in a God so bad as all that? The Cosmic Sadist, the spiteful imbecile? . . . I think it is, if nothing else, too anthropomorphic." (35)

"Real" questions often begin as critical questions that challenge basic modes of thought, definitions, and axioms. They attempt rationally to reevaluate what has been too readily accepted or assumed. Lewis, for example, critiques the faith that is troubling him by bringing to bear upon it strict logical, rational questions, asked not from the perspective of belief, but from an assumed perspective of skepticism: "Sooner or later I must face the question in plain language. What reason have we, except our own desperate wishes, to believe that God is, by any standard we can conceive, 'good'?" (33-34) Real critical questions have to be distinguished, however, from nonsense questions--merely rhetorical exercises that lead to nothing new. This includes recognizing that some questions are not only unanswerable, but useless even to ask. Lewis reflects, for instance,

> Can a mortal ask questions which God finds unanswerable? Quite easily, I should think. All nonsense questions are unanswerable. How many hours are there in a mile? Is yellow square or round? Probably half the questions we ask--half our great theological and metaphysical problems--are like that. (81)

He critiques his own questions even as he asks them. In the midst of speculations about life after death he wonders, "Didn't people dispute once whether the final vision of God was more an act of intelligence or of love?" and then responds, "That is probably another of the nonsense questions" (89).

When critical questions have broken open old habits of thought, reconstructive questions gather together the data of experience for a new synthesis. The autobiographer can become investigator, interrogating his memory in order to reconstruct what happened. This is a non-analytical stage of questioning. The essential question asked is "What happened?" The answers provide a plot outline for the life story.

A further stage in questioning is the formation of integrative questions: questions that provide terms in which the data of experience can be reformed in a new way. When Handke begins to reconstruct his mother's life story in terms of her death, framing the story by asking, what are the roots of despair? he provides in that question a lens through which the whole story takes on different proportions. Every particular of the life, seen in terms of the death it led to, assumes new significance.

Finally, there are generative questions that open up possibilities. These are often left open at the conclusion of a book, pointing the way to uncharted and yet unexplored territories--reminders that conclusions are always only waystations, and that some questions can never be answered conclusively. As Wiesel says, "The questions remain; the answers change."[7] Pirsig makes this concession in his final reflections at the end of *Zen:* he thinks back upon the causes and consequences of his schizophrenia and asks, "But who did it? didn't do it. And there's no way now of undoing it. . . . I keep wondering how far it is to the bottom of that ocean out there. . . " (363). As different stages in questioning reflect different needs, so different kinds of questions produce different answers. "What," "when," and "where" questions yield facts; "why" questions yield speculations; "how" questions trace connections. The thematic patterns of an autobiography can be traced in terms of what question are being posed. The more levels of questioning, the more complicated the narrative produced.

At least two kinds of discourse interweave in any autobiography: the "credo" or discursive answer, and the "story" or narrative answer to the book's central questions. The credo solidifies, distills, and generalizes. The story expands, branches, and particularizes. The credo is a grounding. The story is an elaboration of possibilities.

Asking and Answering: The Autobiographical Dialogue

In her collection of essays, *The Reader and the Writer*, Christa Wolf includes a brief autobiographical fragment that presents the process of writing as she is currently experiencing it. Entitled "Interview With Myself," the piece is written as a dialogue. It is a document of self-exploration written to clarify her own objectives and motives as she works on her semiautobiographical novel, *The Search for Christa T.*. It begins simply: "Q. What are you reading? A. The first pages of a new story I am working on . . "[8] Assigning herself both roles, questioner and answerer, she proceeds to explore the difficulties and possibilities in her project, leading herself to broad questions such as "Why do you think it will interest others?. . . Do you believe literature to be vital? . . . Is there not a contradiction between [the] aim and the actual result?" (78-79)

A Model Childhood extends and complicates this technique. The writer casts herself in multiple roles as narrator (first person), protagonist (second person), and subject (third person), putting the first two into dialogue in order to arrive at a fuller view of the third. Wolf's questions about her past self become a means of exploring and articulating her present inner life. Though *A Model Childhood* seems unusual and even idiosyncratic in its deliberate and self-conscious use of questions and answers, it simply makes more apparent and schematic a process endemic to all autobiography, if not all writing.

Commenting upon the healing aspects of writing, Progoff claims that the dialogue format makes the unconscious accessible in a peculiarly direct way: in the encounter between two assumed personae--the inquiring and the answering selves--something new, a third aspect of self, emerges.[9] This process can bring to light unacknowledged things that hide and fester, repressing truths and causing sickness. Since all autobiography entails this dialectical process, it is useful to examine autobiographies as inner dialogues, to understand how dialogue becomes a dynamic principle in narration.

The most obvious dichotomy in any autobiography is the division between present and past selves. The dialectical relationship between these two aspects of self is most apparent in works like *Of Woman Born* or *Testament of Youth*, where excerpts of earlier writings are juxtaposed with current observations. The contrast between pre-war and post-war perspectives in *Testament of Youth* can be schematized as an internal dialogue: Did my experience mean anything? It is difficult to see what. Is there a lesson to be learned? If there was, it wasn't necessarily worth the price paid for the learning. The alternation of present and past voices keeps the process of evaluation and judgment of experience in flux. The gain in perspective over time is attended by a recognition of loss. The voice of her past self is a reminder of a certain kind of vitality that if she cannot regain, she can at least respect and cherish. Like Wolf, Brittain comes to terms with her past dialectically. Like Rich, she holds up her past self as a case study of the kinds of blindness and repression women submit to and perpetuate.

Autobiographical dialogue can be constructed along other lines. As present self can be set against past self, so the inner and the outer selves can become dialectical poles. Schism between inner and outer life is both an indication of the need for reintegration and, paradoxically, a division necessary to the autobiographical act. (One writer goes so far as to claim that the act of writing by definition demands a kind of schizophrenic perspective.[10]) When an autobiographer distinguishes between these two levels of life, he is measuring the distance between thought and action that autobiography attempts to bridge.

One aim of autobiography is to bring the two selves into harmony by articulating their differences and placing them in a consciously defined relationship. Both Rich and Wolf describe radical differences between their perceptions and behavior that contravened those perceptions, thus tracing the history of deep self-divisions they have come to recognize as wounds that need healing. Rich sees that division as a result of the body-mind dichotomy, which she regards as a disastrous self-violation--one that so commonly tyrannizes women that they can rarely identify the roots of their common depressions and angers. Naming the sources and effects of division is the first step toward healing it. She writes:

> When I try to return to the body of the young woman of twenty-six, pregnant for the first time, who fled from the physical knowledge of her pregnancy and at
> the same time from her intellect and vocation, I realize that I was effectively alienated from my real body and my real spirit by the institution--not the fact--of motherhood. This institution . . . allowed me only certain views, certain expectations. . . (20)

Wolf recalls a similar kind of self-alienation as one of the effects of training in the orthodoxy of Nazism. Constantly called upon in public situations to reinterpret her immediate impressions and resist her instinctive judgments, she gradually lost touch with her own emotional center. Only in retrospect has she been able to recognize the full impact of what she witnessed She asks herself,

> What did Nelly feel when she heard the news of the Binder family's death, in April, 1945, in the village of Gruenheide near Nauen? Loathing? Horror? Dread? Nothing of the kind. Much later, in the midst of other activities which seemed to be demanding her full attention, the neglected feelings caught up with her. (207)

The feeling response to events long past only now emerges, in the act of remembering and reconstructing those events. The autobiography thus provides the writer with a single channel through which the divided currents of the self can mingle. If autobiographers are successful in the quest for sources, they may arrive where those divisions started and regain a sense of the possibility of integrity.

Autobiographical dialogue does not always take the form of direct confrontation of self with self. Sometimes autobiography is a story of relationship. Sometimes the self is a protagonist confronting an Other as antagonist. An archetypal example is Job's dialogue with God. Though not an autobiographical text itself, the book of Job provides a paradigm for certain kinds of autobiography. Both Wiesel and Lewis make explicit reference to it as a model. Wiesel writes, "I prefer to take my place on the side of Job, who chose questions and not answers, silence and not speeches. . . . Only afterward, when he identified himself with his pain, did he feel he had earned the right to question God."[11] Casting God as antagonist makes these autobiographies, like "Job," presentations of a case against God. Both Wiesel and Lewis also use the metaphor of God on trial in later works (Wiesel's *Zahlmen, or the Trial of God* and Lewis's *God in the Dock*), and that situation is implicit in the autobiographies as well. Though God seems to have deserted the authors, they speak into the silence as though he is there and listening.

Sometimes voices of the dead figure in the autobiographical dialogue. Brittain, Lewis, Handke, and Wiesel all write about the loss of someone so integrally related to them that their very selves are defined in some measure by those relationships. Healing from those losses means two things: accepting the dead as dead, and finding a way to make a new relationship with them through memory and writing that allows the writer to stop longing for what was and begin to create something actual and positive.

Wolf and Pirsig both use their children as partners in dialogue. The children function in two ways: they are an audience to whom the writers feel an urgent obligation to communicate clearly; they are also questioners, raising some of the most crucial questions the autobiographers need to ask. When Chris Pirsig asks his father, "Did you ever see a ghost?" the story of Phaedrus is introduced. The answer the author gives his son is cryptic: "I knew a fellow once who spent all his whole life doing nothing but hunting for a ghost, and it was just a waste of time. . . . Then he became a ghost himself" (32-33). But Phaedrus's story is begun in that reply; the question has broken open the Pandora's box of memories, and what is not told to the child, who continues to pose crucial questions, is told to the anonymous reader. The child's questions are catalytic.

Wolf's conversations with her daughter in *A Model Childhood* function similarly. From her limited adolescent perspective, Lenka asks some of the questions most difficult for her mother to answer, and in so doing spurs her mother to deeper self-examination. Wolf wonders how "to be able to reply truthfully to Lenka's questions"--questions like "How can one go on living 'after that?'" (179). The mother reflects:

> While you tell her, you feel that things are not getting any clearer, but rather more confused. You feel the emphasis shifting continuously to issues which are being formed as you speak.
>
> How can you make Lenka understand . . . (180)

Successful communication requires translation. The experience of one person, or of one generation, can only be transmitted in modified terms to another. That process of modification is the "making useful" that Brittain defines as the purpose of autobiography.

The dialectical quality of autobiographical texts counterposes two different modes of discourses: expository and narrative. These form the usual axes of autobiography--a documentary form that combines fact and fiction, history and speculation, statement and story. Handke's *A Sorrow Beyond Dreams* offers a graphic example of alternating modes. The writer frequently pauses midstream to reflect upon the story he is telling. In the very center of the text Handke raises a critical eyebrow at his storytelling:

> These two dangers--the danger of merely telling what happened and the danger of a human individual becoming painlessly submerged in poetic sentences--have slowed down my writing, because in every sentence I am afraid of losing my balance. This is true of every literary effort, but especially in this case, where the facts are so overwhelming that there is hardly anything to think out. (28-29)

Critic jostles storyteller, as two separate aspects of the authorial identity. Each answers the other: critical speculations qualify the narration; narrative reasserts the possibility of transformation through storytelling.

In a sense, all narrative is the product of dialogue. A narrative moves by the impetus of questions, whether implicit or explicit: What happened then? And then? Why? How? On a deeper level, narration is part of a larger ongoing dialogue as well. All literature comes into being by means of this dialectical impetus. Harold Bloom makes the dialectical nature of the literary act explicit in *The Anxiety of Influence* where he argues that every act of writing is a reaction or response to what has been previously written. In form and in use of language, each of these autobiographical texts participates in an ongoing meta-conversation on the nature of autobiography. Each of them attempts to do something new with the form in order to open and address questions that couldn't arise in existing conventional forms of narration, since every convention is based on assumptions and givens which themselves eventually need to be questioned.

Story and Statement: Two Kinds of Answers

When Elie Wiesel is asked a difficult question about his convictions, he frequently responds, "Let me tell you a little story." In the tradition of great religious teachers, Wiesel speaks in parables. Stories generate analogies and possibilities. They do not demand that the listener concede an argument or accept a proposition, but that he consider, apply, and compare the situation presented in the story to his own. Stories are invitations.

Life stories are one way of answering philosophical questions that every individual must confront. They are accounts of action that constitute statements of belief. The way one has lived is measured against (and becomes a measure of) the way one ought to live. Those two axes--what ought to be and what has been--intersect in the present moment of the autobiographical act. Narrative and argument are necessarily intertwined in autobiography, which is always essentially about how things happened and why. The how and the why generate two different kinds of discourse. Together these two reveal a great deal about the autobiographer's understanding of his story and its relationship to the general concerns of humanity. Narrative strategies answer the basic question of how thought and action are related. If story and statement conflict, the effect is ironic. Sometimes the story serves to underscore the argument. Sometimes an argument proceeds inductively from facts presented in the story. In each case, two rhetorical strands intertwine to form a single answer to the questions the autobiographer poses. *Zen and the Art of Motorcycle Maintenance* begins as a story--a travel narrative. The opening sentences establish time, place, and situation:

> I can see by my watch, without taking my hand from the left grip of the cycle, that it is eight-thirty in the morning. The wind,

> even at sixty miles an hour, is warm and humid. When it's this hot and muggy at eight-thirty, I'm wondering what it's going to be like in the afternoon . (3)

A number of facts are given in those lines. The exactitude of the description, and its economy, suggest a speaker with a clear sense of what is important to the story at hand, interested in reporting only what is relevant, and focused upon the immediate. We are located in the present tense, with the narrator on the moving cycle. With the "I'm wondering," a certain intimacy between narrator and reader is implied or at least promised. The narrator continues with a more detailed description of the situation, and of himself. All the basic narrative questions--what, when, where, and how--arise on the first page.

On the second page, facts expand by associations: "For me this is all mixed with memories that [my son] doesn't have." (4) Personal history adds a time dimension to the description of an immediate scene. Things described assume not only shape, but significance.

Then a third dimension appears:

> You see things vacationing on a motorcycle in a way that is completely different from any other. In a car you're always in a compartment. . . . On a cycle the frame is gone. You're completely in contact with it all. You're *in* the scene, not just watching it anymore, and the sense of presence is overwhelming. (4)

Here the poles of an argument begin to take shape: the contrast between cycle and car suggests a number of possible applications. The difference between observation and participation begins to emerge as a theme. The speaker's identity as a cyclist positions him in the ensuing polemic, suggesting what values he attaches to the ideas of "framed" and "unframed" relationships to the world.

The narrator draws the lines of discourse explicitly a few pages later, when he candidly announces his strategy. Continuing the fiction that a reader sits with him on his motorcycle, where, since you can't converse, "you spend your time being aware of things and meditating upon them," he declares that time of inwardness separate from the narrative time of the travel story:

> We're in such a hurry most of the time we never get much chance to talk. . . . Now that we do have some time, and know it, I would like to use the time to talk in some depth about things that seem important.
>
> What is in mind is a sort of Chautauqua . . . like the travelling tent-show Chautauquas that used to move across America, *this* America, the one that we are now in, an old-time series of popular talks intended to edify and entertain, improve the mind and bring culture and enlightenment to the ears and thoughts of the hearer. (7)

Narrative and discursive modes are separated here. This dichotomy is reflected in the metaphor of the trip, with its alternating periods of action and meditation, and in the already established alternation between description of surroundings and of the inner landscape.

Chautauquas present a continuing informal philosophical disquisition on a number of themes: the dichotomizing tendency of the Western mind, the split between romantic and classic world views, language and its limitations, the notion of Quality, the idea of goodness. Once these questions enticed and enthralled the narrator, driving him literally to distraction. One reason they drove him mad, we learn, was the inflexible, dispassionate, and insistently rational method by which he attempted to answer them. Here he attempts to address the same questions in a more creative way. Narrative--storytelling--is the humanizing factor. This time he attends to the subjective, the non-rational, the experiential as well as to the demands of logic and intellectual rigor. The process of finding answers becomes as much a focus as the answers found--becomes, in fact, the more important theme. What has changed since Phaedrus's mad pursuit of answers to cosmic questions is his understanding of the relative importance of process and result. Process is more important. And this shift of values is reflected in the decision to write an autobiographical narrative rather than a philosophical treatise.

How the travel narrative is related to the "inquiry into values" leaves much room for speculation. Yet on one level the trip is clearly a metaphorical enactment of the mental journey mapped in the Chautauquas. Just as the rider must stop and check and sometimes repair his cycle, so the philosopher must stop at intervals to question his own methods, define his terms, and reframe his questions.

In *Of Woman Born* we see a similar interweaving of two distinct modes of discourse, where personal narrative is used as a critique of so-called "objective" scholarship. Adrienne Rich implicitly questions any claim to authority not based on experience. Autobiography is thus an alternative to more broadly based methods of investigating human experience. By choosing it, she claims for personal history validity equal to other forms of statement. Like Anais Nin, Rich believes, and implies, that "the personal life deeply lived" is a valid and important means of approaching general truths, and a necessary complement to intellectual systems that tend to lose touch with the truths of the heart. Only by maintaining the subjective, the experiential, the contextual, can intellectual structures be humanized.

The book opens with sections from her journal detailing the rending ambivalence she experienced as a young mother. Then, abruptly, she makes a transition from intimate narrative to argument with the paragraph heading: "Unexamined assumptions." The diarist suddenly becomes critic: a voice from the past is countered by the present voice, and change is measured in the distance between the two.

Both argument and story are ways of answering Rich's central question, "What was it like for women?" She questions the assumptions and claims of traditional scholarship as well as the methods by which institutionalized forms are perpetuated. Her method is to probe the silences in public discourse, trying to ask the questions left unasked, and to find the "right questions" by measuring discrepancies between her own experience and the cultural myths about women's lives and purposes.

For Rich, as for many feminists, exploration of public questions by means of personal narrative is in itself an assertion: personal stories matter. They are at least as valid a way of finding and presenting general truths as any "objective" scholarly method. The ideal of academic detachment is seriously questioned in her decision to sustain a serious discussion of cultural history by telling an intimate life story. The very categories, "objective" and "subjective" become suspect. Rich strenuously opposes the tendency to dichotomize knowledge in this way. She countermands the dichotomizing impulse by merging narrative and argument, personal and impersonal, particular and general. She is quite explicit about her intention in doing so:

> My own story, which is woven throughout this book, is only one story. What I carried away in the end was a determination to heal--insofar as an individual woman can--the separation between mind and body. . . . Slowly I came to understand the paradox contained in 'my' experience of motherhood; that, although different from many other women's experiences, it was not unique; and that only in shedding the illusion of my uniqueness could I hope, as a woman, to have any authentic life at all. (22)

The lines of demarcation between body and mind, individual and communal life, are blurred.

Rich's literary decisions are also moral decisions; she writes in the service of the things she believes in: awareness, community, female liberation. Like Pirsig, she questions categories of thought because she is deeply concerned about the moral constrictions those categories enforce.

In *A Model Childhood*, personal history also becomes philosophical inquiry. Wolf raises not one, but many questions in her "interrogation of the past"; questions appear like signposts throughout the text. Each question leads author and reader deeper into the past and into wider speculation--and raises more questions. The questions focus not only upon the past, but also upon the present--not only upon the life but also upon the autobiographical process. And each question produces a story. While she digresses into more speculative philosophizing, the author realizes that authentic answers to her searching questions come not as rational demonstrations but as personal stories. "Does memory prefer to store anecdotes?" she wonders. "Something about the structure of memory seems to lend itself to a story with a point" (359).

Like Rich and Pirsig, Wolf uses two modes of discourse to reinforce the dialectical polarities she wants to find and dissolve. She is alternately autobiographer and critic--telling her story and drawing back from it to question the terms in which it is told. This extreme self-consciousness effectively qualifies any mode of narration that lays too heavy a claim to truth or objectivity. There are many different ways to answer any question we ask ourselves, she suggests, and she demonstrates this by asking a series of searching, difficult questions about her own past and her nation's history, and by answering them in defiantly unorthodox terms.

Her first question is one asked on her visa application as she prepares to take a trip back to her childhood home: "Purpose of trip?" "The true answer," she writes, "'research' or 'memory test'--would have raised eyebrows" (4). Like Pirsig's motorcycle journey, her trip is an analogue as well as a preparation for the autobiography. She enters upon both with mixed motives and a sense of risk, knowing more than many the risks of questioning, her childhood having been spent in an atmosphere where many questions were better left unasked.

Wolf's central question is one that demands a narrative answer: "How did we become what we are?" That question raises others: What are the roots of change? Which is more powerful--the inner impulse or the pressure from without? Where does moral responsibility begin --and end?

She seeks her answer by reaching back to her earliest recollections of independent thought to that moment on the front steps when the child that was herself sat repeating the pronoun, "I . . . I . . . I . . ." with a sense of discovery and secrecy that was the beginning of her inner life. She asks to what end the child began to lead that separate, inner existence, and reflects,

"The question is as ominous as it is justified. . . . The feeling that overcomes any living being when the earth starts moving underfoot is fear" (24).

A second thematic question--"How does memory function?"--leads her not only to examine the past, to identify the moments of change and trace connections, but also to scrutinize the process by which she is bringing that past to light. How does one avoid self-deception, she asks, when its roots go so deep? As she examines the self-deceptions in her past, rooting out and exposing festering guilt and identifying unasked questions, the narrator insistently reminds herself how ever-present the temptation is to deceive herself once again by leaving the most disturbing questions unasked. Like Lewis, she finds authorial power disturbing because of the ease with which she might indulge in self-protective distortions.

> Why are you more disturbed by the fact that all of these people are at your mercy? Take Charlotte. She can't protest, can't rectify or mend anything, can't correct the word 'triumph' if she finds it wrong. You can say what you want about her, whatever comes to mind. (200)

Again in Chapter 10 she questions the morality of her presumed authority to reshape the past:

> Aren't you fooling yourself by thinking that this child is moving on her own, according to her own inner laws? Living within preconceived patterns--that's the problem. . . . The child is your vehicle the moment she starts humming. To what purpose? (210)

"Incidentally, what do words like 'deep' and 'shallow' mean in relation to memory?" (153) "Is remembering tied to action? It would explain their loss of memory, for they didn't act" (154). The process is insistently two-directional: the further she descends into the past, the more deeply and critically she delves into the complex workings of her own authorial psyche.

She tries to ask the "right" questions, and to identify what are the wrong questions that divert and confuse and fail to enlighten: "Why didn't they suffer? The question is wrong . . ." (156). Finding the right questions involves a painstaking redefinition of terms:

> You ask yourselves why the conviction that man should be guided by his knowledge, rather than by his faith, has thus far produced so little beauty. You find no answer, because the question is posed wrongly. It doesn't cover the type, the extent, the direction, and the goal of this knowledge. (338)

This is why Wolf finds it so difficult to answer her daughter's questions at times. In her ignorance, the child does not know how to ask the "right" questions. Some questions can only be asked from within an experience. From outside, some actions are not only incomprehensible, but inexplicable. "How can you make Lenka understand," she wonders, "that Nelly's childhood continued colorfully, beyond these issues?" (180)
"Who wouldn't wish to have a happy childhood?" Wolf asks (25). The question is in part a warning to herself: through writing she is in a position to fulfill that wish--to create a fictional childhood for herself. But her business is to separate truth from fiction, if that is possible, and to answer the questions memory raises rather than continue to avoid them. So she begins painstakingly to recall facts: places and incidents and people. "Who is interested in these people," she asks--"Why go on with the list of the dead?" The importance of the facts she dredges up is not immediately apparent. Purpose gets buried in detail. The diver must keep going back under the surface. It is hard to stay there. The surface is where life is carried on, and where the findings can be examined.

The narrator is not the only questioner. The questions that come from her daughter, while often asked in ignorance, spur her to probe deeply to find ways of answering them, if only by rephrasing. In her innocence, Lenka asks hard questions that penetrate to the sore spots guilt has left and lays a burning finger on them: "What does it really mean, Polack, Lenka wants to know. She's never heard the word, 'Polack,' or the saying 'dumb as a Polack' . . . 'dirty Polack' . . . Does she have to know them?" Wolf is not only an author, but a mother. She reflects upon herself not only as a figure in the drama of her own past, but as an agent in the transmission of an ambiguous legacy. Motherhood raises its own set of questions: "Will your attitude someday seem strange to her," she asks herself, "the same way the attitude of the preceding generation seemed strange to you?" (30)

The author reflects upon herself also as daughter. She wonders what her own mother would say of her enterprise. "If you could ask her," she thinks, "Charlotte would probably say: Do what you must. Not quite the sentence you'd like to hear. Better: Do it if you must. But how can you know with absolutely certainty what you must do?" (34) Every relationship poses a question for her, giving her someone to answer to for some particular aspect of her life and work, and also reinforces her separateness, reminding her of the loneliness of the autobiographical quest.

Her first chapters are about people who refrained from asking questions. They took at face value the promises and rationalizations the German government offered them, as one by one their freedoms were curtailed. Subtle threats forced them to blind themselves or stifle their objections to the myriad injustices they witnessed as the insidious policies of the Third Reich gained a foothold in their daily lives. She recalls how unquestioningly her parents and their friends accepted published news at face value: "Any other information did not concern them" (37). She remembers an ex-prisoner, astonished at her mother's gullibility, saying, "Where on earth have you all been living." She reflects on his words:

> He wasn't asking a question. He didn't have the strength for one. In those days, a marked lack of strength and trust and insight . . . may have rendered certain possibilities of German grammar temporarily inoperative. Interrogative, declarative, or exclamatory sentences could no longer--or not yet--be used. Many, Nelly among them, lapsed into silence. Many muttered softly to themselves, shaking their heads. Where did you live. What did you do. What's going to happen now--things like that. (39)

"Nelly's" history could be read as a counterpoint between asked and unasked questions. The author traces her development in terms of the questions she asked or decided not to. She recalls how carefully she was trained as a child not to ask certain questions: "Had her curiosity . . . diminished?" she wonders. "Does curiosity diminish if it remains unsatisfied for a long time? Is it possible to numb a child's curiosity completely?" She measures her own experience of this gradual suffocation against what she has heard about how people live under dictatorship: "They learn to restrict their curiosity to realms that are not dangerous to them. . . " and she thinks, "It should be asked: Isn't it the nature of curiosity to be preserved either in its entirety or not at all?" (67) One of the purposes of the autobiographical enterprise is to revive and satisfy the questioning faculty--to test the strength of the curiosity that might have been killed off--the humanizing instinct to seek awareness.

Again and again the narrator identifies points at which her curiosity was damped or threatened, times she resisted asking questions. "It seems evident," she writes,

> that children don't wish to know everything about their parents. Nelly was possessed by a more than average inquisitiveness and was forced during her entire childhood to hide this precious trait, even from herself, to the point where it was in danger of being stifled. But she didn't have the slightest wish to hear anything disparaging about her parents. (123)

To ask is now her business--but a difficult one. More difficult because some questions have remained unasked for so long, it is difficult even to discover what they are. The child's history is presented as a history of unasked questions. The writing of her story is the asking of those questions, and the story is also the answer.

Inconclusion

Vita Sackville-West once remarked, "I have come to the conclusion, after many years of sometimes sad experience, that you cannot come to any conclusion at all."12 This observation is particularly true of autobiography, by definition an open-ended form. The autobiographer's story is subject to change as long as he is alive, for, as Eliot trenchantly observed, the present changes the past. The questions autobiography answers need to keep being asked as one's perspective continues to change. Progoff claims that if one were to perform the exercise each year of dividing one's life into "chapters," the divisions would be different each time.13 Every change involves a kaleidescopic shift; "There's no way to change," one poet has written, "without touching/the space at the center of everything."14

The answers autobiography offers are therefore necessarily inconclusive. If one's life is evidence of anything, it is at best incomplete evidence. Autobiography presents itself not as *the* answer, but only as one among many possible answers to the questions life keeps raising. As the context shifts, both questions and answers must be reformulated.

If it is true, as E.D. Hirsch once observed, that every book is an answer to a question,15 it is surely also true that a good book raises as many questions as it purports to answer. To go on living is to go on seeking and questioning. It is a common convention for modern autobiographers to end inconclusively, on a seventh chord, to remind the reader that resolution, like stability, is at best momentary--a precarious balance point, a vantage point, that must in its turn be left behind.

The last words of *A Sorrow Beyond Dreams* are a refusal to conclude: "Someday I shall write about all this in greater detail." The questions Handke has raised about his own grief and the process of living and writing it out, and about his mother's life, have not been answered--or the answers have only been a few among many possible answers. Time will offer new perspectives.

Similarly, Christa Wolf concludes with an admission of inconclusiveness: "I shall not revolt against the limits of the expressible." The rest is silence. The answers language can formulate are inevitably incomplete, for every formulation is only one camera-angle on the many-sided realities. The real questions--the right questions--the questions that are the province of truth seekers--are finally unanswerable, though they must be asked. Autobiography validates itself as a form in its very admission of contingency and its limited claims to truth. An autobiography is *a* truth about *a* life--one story among many possible stories--one version of the human story--one answer to the overwhelming questions that continue to arise again and again, always demanding that new answers be found, or old answers be made new.

---

[1] Richard Church, "The Art of Autobiography,"*Cornhill* 171 (1960-61), p. 474.

[2] Burke, p. 1.

[3] Cargas, p. 58.

[4] Robert A. Lloyd, *Images of Survival* (New York: Dodd, Mead and Co., 1973), p. 35.

[5] Elie Wiesel, *Legends*, p. 222.

[6] Carol Gilligan recounted this experience in a Gauss Seminar lecture at Princeton University in October, 1982.

[7] Cargas, p. 105.

[8] Christa Wolf, *The Reader and the Writer (Lesen und Schreiben)*, trans. Joan Becker (New York: International Publishers, 1977), p. 76.

[9] Ira Progoff, *Journal*. See especially Chapter 3.

[10] Neil Simon, "Portrait of the Writer as Schizophrenic" in the introduction to *Collected Plays of Neil Simon* (New York: Random House, 1971), pp. 3 ff.

[11] Wiesel, *Legends*, p. 221.

12 Vita Sackville-West, quoted in *A Woman's Notebook* (Philadelphia: Running Press, 1980), p. 30.

13 Progoff made this claim at an Intensive Journal Workshop given in Palo Alto, California, in 1978.

14 Chana Bloch, "Firewood," in *The Secrets of the Tribe* (New York: Sheep Meadow Press, 1981), p. 58.

15 E.D. Hirsch, *Validity in Interpretation*, introduction.

CHAPTER 5

FORMING AND TRANSFORMING

Autobiography and the Question of Form

Psychologist Robert Lifton claims that our century has produced a peculiar breed of person he calls "protean man." In an age of radical diversity, schism, and atomization, the life of a "protean man"

> is characterized by easy shifts in beliefs and identifications rooted in endless searching, exploration, and flux in all areas of human experience. He can rather easily identify with a variety of beliefs, ideas, and symbols but he has immense difficulty sustaining any prolonged allegiance or connection with these.[1]

Such persons also retain a persistent sense of "the absence of 'fit' between inner and outer worlds."[2] Lifton's analysis sheds a certain light on the changing function and forms of autobiography, and suggests why so many modern autobiographies are experimental in form, why so many focus on discrepancies between inner and outer reality, and why so many express a need to recover some form of lost coherence.

If we are living protean lives, the stories we tell about those lives can hardly pretend to definitive status; no narrative structure can fully accomodate a shifting, formless, many-levelled reality. We are more aware than ever that "stories and lives are not the same thing," that the shape of an autobiography is not the shape of the life, but an artful recasting of the raw material life provides. Authorial responsibility is therefore greater, as authors tell their life stories not so much to reconfirm an established pattern (as in conversion narratives) as to find modes of presentation that assert uniqueness and suggest new ways of defining the relationship between inner and outer worlds. Pluralism and deinstitutionalization imply endless variation. Autobiographies are a natural product of such conditions.

Just as psychology has produced a wide variety of models of the self, so the impact of those models has manifested itself in literary experimentation, particularly in autobiography. Not only has autobiography proliferated, but it has appeared in a myriad of new and hybrid forms. Robert Sayre has observed that "We cannot talk about concepts of the self . . . without realizing that those concepts inevitably take different literary forms as well as different social and cultural ones."[3] The autobiographer's task is to give the "protean self" form, center, and shape in narrative.

Some of the most poignant lines in Adrienne Rich's poem, "The Insomniacs," describe the situation of the autobiographer trying to express in language the inchoate and inarticulate truths of the inner life:

> My voice controls the formal stage;
> A jungle thrives beyond the wings--
> All formless and benighted things
> That rhetoric cannot assuage.[4]

The writer's vocation is to bring those "formless and benighted things" into the light of consciousness, drawing them into the syntax of common experience. For the autobiographer, the "formless thing" is his or her own life. Rich is one of many modern writers who have realized the dangers of falsification inherent in a too-facile imposition of preconceived patterns upon experience. She realizes that many truths go untold because there is no place for them in traditional narrative structures. Her work, as she defines it, is to find ways of telling those untold truths.[5] To do that means acknowledging that life is not neatly shaped; it offers few moments of complete resolution or closure. Rich thus speaks of her poetic growth as "coming to terms with the untidiness of reality.[6]

Since it is impossible to see life whole, we frame it and shape it with psychological, mythic, and literary modes that give it an appearance of coherence. But forms and systems are only containers into which to pour that fluid substance of life; sometimes it overflows them. Conventional forms of expression suddenly appear hopelessly inadequate, and one must venture into the "jungle beyond the wings" not yet domesticated by language.

Until recently, a fairly stable set of myths and paradigmatic stories have provided models for Western autobiography. The Greek tales of quest and conquest, the Christian story of death and rebirth, conversion stories, chivalric tales of heroism and transforming loves have provided prototypes for life stories--conventions that autobiographers have adapted variously in different ages, according to changing cultural and individual needs.

In the years following World War I the disintegration of cultural institutions, including formative mythologies that feed the common imagination, reached such a degree that those patterns came to be perceived not only as artificial, but as spurious and falsifying. They no longer seemed usable vehicles for expressing the kinds of truth that needed telling about modern lives. As the mythic substructure of our culture has become increasingly qualified, ironized, and hence weakened, we are less and less governed by the imperatives implied in strong models. Normative stories lose their moral force; we tend to idealize innovation rather than imitation. Moral relativism has undermined our models--we are not a hero-worshipping generation--and reduced our myths to self-conscious fictions. Since we are no longer so closely bound by prescriptive norms, a greater burden of choice devolves upon the individual to define the norms he will live by, and, correspondingly, upon an individual author to find a way of turning life into a story that sets him apart. The Romantic ideal of fidelity to the inner self has achieved the status of a moral imperative. Autobiography valorizes heterodoxy: individuals must shape reality to their own designs.

This Romantic heritage accounts in part for the wide-ranging experiments in psychological mimesis since the 1920's. "Protean" life naturally generates a multiplicity of literary forms and styles. With the disappearance of prescriptive models, autobiographies have tended to become less formulaic, more organic. The archetypal patterns that shape experience are less determinative because we can stand critically outside them and perceive them as artificial.

Janet Varner Gunn describes the dialectical struggle between raw experience and archetypal forms as a "process of 'schema and correction' which not only characterizes experience but makes it available to us as our own."[7] One's life story is thus a compromise between experience and preconceived pattern. This process of examining old stories and "correcting" them assumed radical form among the post-World War I modernists. By fragmenting and recombining traditional forms and conventions, Eliot, Pound, H.D., and others reacted to cultural disintegration by creating literary forms that would accomodate a more complex view of reality. Susan Friedman writes that H.D., for instance, "experimented with a variety of genres in her search for the writing that could fix the unending process of self-becoming in the temporary status of a text."[8] William Spengemann goes so far as to claim that "the very idea of literary modernism seems synonymous with that of autobiography."[9]

Brittain reacted to the challenge to find new and truer forms of expression with modernist eclecticism. In *Testament of Youth*, Brittain uses, and implicitly criticizes, virtually all the classic literary forms, turning them to her purposes ironically, exposing their limitations, showing where their correspondences to lived life break down. Like her contemporaries, Brittain saw herself as living in the ruins of a shattered world, unable any longer to aspire to a Romantic ideal of perfection or wholeness. The perceived insufficiency of all existing systems of thought resulted in the common conviction that there is no arriving at whole truth, absolutes, nor any wholly reliable vantage point: one can only perceive reality from discrete and limited perspectives. That being so, the only viable approach to "wholeness" seemed to be to bring together various perspectives to create a composite mosaic. Through this formal technique, modernist texts invite a reader to reconsider the nature of narrative authority by focusing attention on variables in the act of composition rather than fostering an illusion of consistency.

One way of expressing a modern philosophy of literary form is the maxim, "there are no truths, only narrative structures." What Brittain created in *Testament of Youth* is a narrative structure in which the fragmentary and slippery nature of truth is foregrounded. In its form alone the text tells an important truth: that truth is not one, but manifold, complex, and even contradictory. She pieces together fragments of recognized literary forms; chameleon-like, the story takes on characteristics of classic tragedy, pastoral, epic, lyric, and elegy, inducing the expectations each raises, only to subvert those expectations in the end.

The first half of *Testament of Youth* seems closely linked to classical tragedy: the story inspires horror and pity; choices made in ignorance lead the protagonist, the young nurse, through anguish to wisdom. Her tragic flaw is innocence. Beginning in that fatal state of innocence, she progresses through stages of disillusionment to enlightenment. Though she suffers almost total loss, the story ends with a promise of regeneration and renewal.

In the tradition of most tragic heroines, Brittain experiences the powerlessness of womanhood as part of her fate. Like so many female figures in tragedy, she comes near madness in the isolation her experience forces upon her. Like them, she is tempted by suicide. Like them, she assumes responsibility for building a new life out of the ruins of the old one, and in doing so transforms failure and despair into heroic action. What raises her to heroic dimensions is her decision to assume responsibility for her own destiny.

Reading *Testament* under the rubric of tragedy highlights the themes of responsibility, choice, and triumph over fate, and discloses a vision of heroism that has more to do with acceptance, adaptation, and compassion than with nationalistic idealism. Brittain creates a new kind of female hero to set against a long tradition of powerful but self-destructive tragic women, from Clytemnestra to Hedda Gabler. Unlike these prototypes, she does not end in self-destruction, but resolves to create a new life. The fulfillment of that resolve lies partly in writing her autobiography.

In subject and treatment the story is also an epic, yet the idea of epic is likewise subverted and transformed. Brittain writes about the traditional epic subject of war in a mode decidedly not "exalted in style" nor "heroic in theme"--two classic requirements of the genre. Her muse is the ghost of her past self, and the questions she asks of it generate a speculative dialogue rather than an authoritative account of events. She shifts the focus from the broad field of action to the inner life of feeling and thought. The loss of human lives in war is exposed as a shameful waste rather than a cause for national pride. If she sings the unsung heroines of that war, she sings in a minor key with many a discordant note, a song that is more a lament than a paean.

In many ways the narrative is elegiac, but elegy is also ironized. Elegy is a form of lamentation, but these lamentations are seasoned with rage. An elegy usually ends peacefully, or even joyfully. But this elegiac voice reminds us, even in the peaceful ending that the book finally achieves, that peace is a still precarious and difficult ideal and that joy is forever undermined by irrevocable loss.

The author's interlude on the island of Malta (Chapter 7) introduces pastoral and lyric elements into the narrative. If, as Empson claimed, the essence of pastoral is "a putting of the complex . . . into the simple, such as a rustic setting,"[10] Brittain's memories of Malta are quintessentially pastoral--they recall an interlude in the war years spent out of the worst of the fray, recovering from the war's confusions and losses in a place of peace: "Wherever we went the spring flowers, lovely and benevolent, mitigated the invisible antagonism of the rocks" (323).

Brittain also draws heavily upon the epistolary novel as a model. Much of the story unfolds through letters exchanged between herself and Roland, adding yet another perspective to the inherent doubleness of the autobiographical form, complicating the reader's task of locating truth somewhere in the field of tension created by the multiple voices.

Each chapter in *Testament* begins with a poem--usually one of Brittain's own or Roland's--written in forms already outmoded by the time she wrote the autobiography. Her poetry and her prose again seem to speak with two different voices--the one a form in which feeling is dominant, and in the other the intellect. The voice of the poet and the voice of the autobiographer are quite distinct, and add yet another dimension to the multiple dialectics of the text.

By calling her work a "testament" or "history," Brittain effectively removes it from any standard literary category. Though she employs literary conventions artfully, the term "history" is her principal generic term. Her decision to write autobiography and use fictional forms asserts that this way of telling history is as legitimate as any other: individual lives deserve attention as much as general ideas formulated by political and cultural historians. Using a hybrid form allows Brittain to undercut conventional reader expectations and forge a relationship between author and reader that demands a nonconventional response.

Yet the structure that evolves out of this experimentation with form is still highly patterned. Brittain's resistance to conventional forms does not produce formlessness. Her story remains formally conservative in its classic symmetry and mythic structure (reinforced by its fairy-tale epigraph). The book consists of three parts, corresponding to three distinct stages in the writer's emotional and intellectual odyssey. Part I says, in effect, "I believed." Part II says, "I was deceived." Part III concludes, "Nevertheless, I will go on." Each part begins with an ending: the ending of the world as she knew it, the death of the man she loved, the end of the war. But each of those endings is a beginning. The last page of the book ends on this note: "I found it not inappropriate that the years of frustration and grief and loss, of work and conflict and painful resurrection, should have led me through their dark and devious ways to this new beginning."

Though the story hardly comes full circle or to complete closure, it retains a satisfying symmetry that offsets fragmentation and offers a familiar reassurance in the end.

Brittain's chronological arrangement, climactic structure, and implicit trust in memory contrast sharply with Christa Wolf's later narrative. In *A Model Childhood* the formlessness of both inner and outer worlds becomes thematic, and the insistence upon the essential unreliability of any statement deeply qualifies the narrator's authority. Wolf deconstructs conventional schemas far more explicitly and self-consciously than Brittain. She treats the issue of form as both a moral and an aesthetic problem. Like Brittain, Wolf writes about a time when the world around her was in a state of chaos, but she also refuses to sustain the fiction that she writes from a stable vantage point. She is constantly aware of the shifting shapes of her own memories and perceptions. She sees truth-telling not only as a problem of breaking through conventions, but of finding a way in writing to remain faithful to all the levels of truth that might be told at any moment. One of her ways of expressing this multivalence is to divide the autobiographical self into three distinct persons or voices, thereby suggesting the complexity of the problems of viewpoint and character.

Aware that any fixed form has inherent limitations, Wolf invents a style of narration that reflects the kaleidescopically shifting relationship between inner and outer worlds, past and present, memory and imagination, experience and idea, factual and fictional events. In this work, autobiography, like documentary and "new journalism," works as a "hybrid" form. By crossing categorical boundaries she works out new ways of describing experience. Since the formal requirements of autobiography are minimal, its possibilities are many. Yet autobiography not only imposes form upon experience, but transforms it as well, by providing a meeting place for factual memory and fictive imagination.

Francis Hart's description of the autobiographical process seems accurately to describe Wolf's technique: Hart sees autobiography as an endlessly generative dialectic between authorial control and submission to the inchoate and inarticulate side of experience:

> Form in an autobiographical work partakes in experimental fluctuation of both control and revelation, and the experimental activity often generates a variety of controlled forms: the tensile forms of inner and outer, man and mask, Dichtung und Wahrheit; forms of stylistic and modal counterpoint; metaphoric or parabolic forms. . .; rhythmic and expository and therapeutic forms; . . . anti-forms playing against conventional expectations. Some of these are manifest experimentally in the emergent narrative patterns of the recovered life. Others appear in the *dramatic* patterns of the evolving act of recovery.[11]

One difficulty in such experimentation is developing valid criteria for selecting and ordering experiences into a coherent pattern without falsifying them. The romantic notion of "organic form" survives perhaps most legitimately in autobiography. As modern autobiographers veer away from received forms toward more idiosyncratic ones, they seek inner principles of organization to give the life shape. Finding such a principle of organization is the first formal problem an autobiographer faces. Once the possibility of whole sight is dismissed, the challenge is to find an angle of vision that provides an integral from which a whole might be derived. Henry James observed that "the whole truth about anything is never told; we can only take what groups together."[12] Yet despite this admission, James was obsessed with the challenge of developing a holistic mode of discourse that would envelop all levels of inner and outer experience.

Things only "group together," of course, in the presence of an organizing principle or constellating image. This principle can lie in the personal motive behind the autobiographical act, or in a didactic purpose. But the multiplicity of events combined with the multiple demands of narrative itself tend to take a writer beyond limits suggested by any preconceived notion of his objectives. Form emerges from an encounter with events that correct the *a priori* schemas that allow us to form a gestalt of those events. Everything the writer writes changes his relationship to his subject. Elizabeth Bruss uses Boswell's journal to illustrate how autobiography thus defies fixity:

> Boswell had certainly hoped that maintaining a journal might change him. But the changes he had hoped to effect--'fixing' himself in a character, 'preserving' his inclinations 'constant and warm'--were intended to bring stability to the uncertain, shifting mass of his identity. Instead of imposing a positive and final form on himself, his journal has become another unknown entailing even greater uncertainty.[13]

If an autobiography is not to become either hagiography or cautionary tale, but to reflect some of the complex truths about life, its organizing principles must be dynamic and organic. Form must somehow reflect process.

A principle of organization constitutes an implicit statement of value. To decide in what terms the story shall be told means defining what is important about the story. One of the results of crisis is radical redefinition of importance. Since in crisis the categories and priorities one has accepted as givens no longer appear inevitable, writing about crisis means recasting them. In Pirsig's terms, one looks for new ways to "wield the analytical knife."

One characteristically modern response to the question of importance is to abdicate moral judgment. Modern vision tends toward the paratactic. Hierarchies seem artificial or even spurious to the modern mind; very few value systems appear self-evident any more. Since values are no longer clearly predefined by consensus, an individual autobiographer must develop and justify his own criteria for selecting and arranging facts into a meaningful pattern. Even writers with urgent moral concerns, such as Wiesel, tend to avoid pointed moralizing. *Night* presents a disjointed series of images, isolated representative moments, associatively connected, that accumulate but do not imply progress toward a culminating epiphany--they simply deepen the horror. The story is told in chronological sequence, but also flattens time by demonstrating the irrelevance of time in the timeless, endlessly repetitive hell of camp life. The narrative reflects a marginal world, where conventional sense-making devices are either removed or ritualized to the point of absurdity. Clearly Wiesel is attempting in his manner of telling to recreate symbolically that sinister and bizarre atmosphere for the reader. To that end he resists the demands of conventional narrative for logical order, closure, and resolution: the niceness of such ordering devices might undermine the horror of the arbitrariness and chaos, might even trivialize and falsify the events described. What happened at Auschwitz must not be too easily explained or grasped. In her analysis of the literature of the Holocaust, Sidra Ezrahi offers an example of the failure of known forms to contain experience:

> The disjunction between generic memory and conventional forms on the one hand and 'millennial ' subject matter and the literary forms which have evolved to contain the new reality on the other, is a measure of the shifts in the boundaries of art beyond which the imagination becomes inarticulate and form disintegrates altogether.[14]

Form, in other words, is meaning. William Howarth describes the autobiographical act as a progression "from motive, to method, to meaning," implying that motive determines form, which then delimits interpretive horizons.[15] The motive of healing produces texts which can be perceived as restorative or redemptive by both reader and writer. In such texts the integrative overcomes the diffusive: connecting principles become evident and believable, yet they remain transparent enough to reveal elements of discovery and surprise in the autobiographical process. Such texts demand to be read as acts--records of an ongoing process--rather than as stable structures. And these texts clearly have fictive elements; possibilities complement facts. In that fictional thrust, Spender writes, "the autobiographical is transformed. It is no longer the writer's own experience: it becomes everyone's. He is no longer writing about himself: he is writing about life.[16]

Form and Meaning

In *A Model Childhood* Christa Wolf notes "how naturally all stories seemed to develop once one knew their ending: as though they had never had the choice to develop differently, to lead to a different fate, to different persons" (386). We want meaning and order to appear inherent in the nature of things. When the structures that reinforce our sense of order begin to appear artificial and even arbitrary, they no longer satisfy that need and must be replaced with structures that correspond more closely to the contours of experience. Hence the search for new forms of narrative.

In a state of crisis, "things fall apart, the center cannot hold." Yeats's words characterize not only the state of the modern world as he prophetically saw it, but serve to describe rather accurately the feeling quality of personal crisis as well. Consciousness of impending chaos demands adaptation. Two kinds of adaptation are possible: to retain a teleological outlook and search for meaning and pattern in more complex paradigms, or to accept the absence of inherent meaning and rely upon the brief self-contained moments instead. Old ideas of continuity, consistency, and sequence become dubious. Narratives of life stories reflect both these adaptations. Both are ways of coping with the loss undergone when old myths and forms lose their power to contain and explain experience.

In his essay, "The Value of Narrativity," Hayden White distinguishes between "narrating" and "narrativizing"--the first being "a discourse that openly adopts a perspective that looks out on the world and reports it," and the second "a discourse that feigns to make the world speak itself and speak itself *as a story* ."[17] It is increasingly difficult to "make the world speak itself" in this way. Less and less do the forms of narrative seem inherent in the nature of things. Existential responsibility implies authorial responsibility. Georges Gusdorf comments upon the responsibility of an author to invent his own narrative structures just as he designs his own life style:

> Today's comprehensive psychology has taught us that man, far from being subject to ready-made, completed situations given from outside and without him, is the essential agent in bringing about the situations in which he finds himself placed. It is his intervention that structures the terrain where his life is lived and gives it its ultimate shape, so that the landscape is truly, in Amiel's phrase, 'a state of the soul.'[18]

Recognition of this uncertainty principle can indeed be a cause of crisis, but it has also been a means by which writers have surmounted crisis. Taking responsibility for "world-making" is the existential challenge: to do so is a powerful way of relating to the world. Authoring a new vision of things is an empowering process.

The problem is finding new forms that allow one to express a new vision of things. New forms are difficult to invent because archetypes possess enormous power. Resisting those archetypes requires extreme self-consciousness: one must dive very deep to find "the thing itself and not the myth."

The problem is that we have only a certain recognized repertoire of forms as available vehicles for communication, and we cannot do without them. As Robert Scholes observed, narrative processes and structures "are too deeply rooted in human physical and mental processes to be dispensed with by members of this species."[19] When available forms do not suffice, we find ourselves in that marginal area of experience analogous to the ends of the sound spectrum: we must invade the formless silence lying beyond the boundaries of language and attempt to domesticate it, like Rich's "jungle beyond the wings."

Modern writers have, of course, made numerous attempts to resist archetypal forms. They have ironized them, as Brittain does in her *Testament*; they have bent them to new uses, as Pirsig does the mythic journey; they have explicitly defied them, as both Handke and Rich do. These writers recognize the conventions and forms that govern us, and attempt to reconstellate them. In that reconstellation the relationship between form and meaning is altered.

Mythic forms can be revalidated by adaptation. Wiesel offers one example of this process in his attempt to link his literary work with Judaic forms of prayer and liturgy. Reiterating Kafka's claim that writing is a "form of prayer," Wiesel adds, "Prayers are of a rich variety. There can be intellectual prayers, long prayers, short prayers, simple prayers."[20] He says of his own works, "I would like them to be a liturgy: chants, prayers, all of them.[21] Reflecting upon these aspirations, he asks,

> What is a prayer? It is a kind of selection of words against others, of the exclusion of some words before others. In doing this you create a zone of piety, a certain zone of expectation, of waiting and of silence which surrounds the prayer and the prayer comes out of itself.[22]

Wiesel's writings secularize and transform the forms of Judaism that structured his life. However, his attempt to infuse those old forms with new meaning is problematic. Ezrahi elucidates this problem in her critique of Wiesel's work: "It seems as if the aesthetic forms and religious categories that are to constitute the shape and substance of Wiesel's fiction cannot be cultivated on a substructure of atrocity."[23] Patterning his stories upon forms of prayer and midrashic tales, she observes, allows him to fuse reality and legend.[24] However problematic this strategy, it links him to a tradition in which he might otherwise have lost his grounding. As Elsbree asserts, even when we have ideologically dismissed our sustaining mythologies, they continue to provide us with forms for our stories. Myths are our "agents of stability" because by building upon mythic patterns, individual stories link to a broad base of human experience and situate the individual within the world in a reassuring way.

Many modern writers see this reassurance as dangerously blinding, however. Langer is very pointed in his attacks on such strategies of reorientation: "The habit of finding old spiritual categories and vocabulary to sanctify the meaningless new deaths (to say nothing of the lucky survivals) of the Holocaust has never seemed to me a fruitful way of entering the darkest recesses of that horror."[25] He bitterly criticizes Viktor Frankl as one of the primary offenders in this questionable endeavor:

> Somehow, the Holocaust must fit into the old world order (as well as the old *word* order), and in his determination to establish such continuity, Frankl narrows the event to the familiar challenge of finding meaning in suffering. But his language blunts the

> menacing blade of atrocity and simplifies the threat of extermination into a conventional encounter between the free heroic spirit and human mortality. The horrors of Auschwitz fade behind a wall of rhetoric. . .26

Meaning-making can be a form of self-protection against the invasion of the chaotic, the unknown, the overpowering. We tend to exclude and ignore what does not fit into our paradigms, because we have no name or category for the anomalous. Langer's observations suggest that, in the case of the Holocaust, it is important not to resort to this kind of self-protective limitation because that would blind us to hard truths and make us susceptible again to the deceptions that generated atrocity. Convention can tend toward dangerous sentimentalization and oversimplification. When all the "ragged edges" have been trimmed off, the resulting gestalt, however reassuring, will leave important truths untold. The "ragged edges" assail us in time of crisis.

For most modern writers, relativity and randomness seem much truer characteristics of reality than ordered hierarchies and progressions. Hence they seek forms that do not fix meaning, but are open-ended. Ezrahi suggests that for those who wrote out of the Holocaust experience, "it may be precisely in its *resistance* to conceptual abstraction, to psychological reductionism, that art as a version of historical memory can provide form without fixing meaning, insight without explanation for the recovered events.27

Peter Handke's *A Sorrow Beyond Dreams* attempts to achieve such "insight without explanation" and to link form to meaning in a loose, open-ended way. The book is about surfaces and interiors, about the difficulty of reaching the truth of things because language pulls us centrifugally toward a periphery. Opposites interweave throughout the book into a form that reflects its underlying philosophical tension. Handke simultaneously tells both a life story and a death story. He brings his mother's life and death (and his own life) together in the epigraph, quoting Bob Dylan: "He not busy being born is busy dying." Portraying reality as a field of interpenetrating opposites, the text is insistently dialectical: it counterpoises journal and biography, the minds of son and mother, words and silences. The final product affirms meaning and exposes the roots of futility. The reconstruction of the life story is also a deconstruction.

The overall structure of Handke's narrative bears out this principle of interpenetration. The book contains five sections: the first and fifth, the second and forth of which are concentric frames that encircle a brief center section--a four-page parenthetical interlude. The result is an interlayering of the writer's journal (the first, third, and fifth sections) with the biographical narrative (the second and fourth sections). The reader moves into that core at the center where the meaning of the "life story" is both explicated and questioned. Those central questions radically alter his reading of the last half of the narrative.

Each of the five sections serves a different purpose. In the first section the writer explains, in the middle section he questions, and in the final section he deconstructs his own project. The first half of the mother's story is about abortive beginnings; the second half about untimely endings. Two modes of perception, two voices, and two forms of writing alternate and modify each other. The life story, Handke shows us, is a surface--a mask on the face of death. By writing he seeks to penetrate that surface--to go behind the facts of his mother's personal history to the inner principles that moved her to self-destruction. He presents her development as a series of adaptations made into increasingly stifling and oppressive circumstances. The strategies she adopted in order to survive ultimately failed her, for they were denials of life, efforts to shrink to the mold cast for her by family and society. Describing them, Handke shows how they finally reduced her to "nothing:" how she became "content to be nothing, or at least nothing much" (34).

In writing the life story, Handke writes against the life. His narrative strategies pointedly invert the survival strategies that killed his mother's desire to live. Where she masked, he unmasks; where she romanticized, he deromanticizes; where she evaded, he confronts; where she accepted and submitted to the inevitable, he assumes and literalizes authorial power and defies fate. By recreating her life as a story, he is even refusing to submit to the finality of her death; instead he makes her death an occasion for restoring life in a different form. The narrative is a corrective to the life.

Whereas the mother lived by closing, contracting, and shrinking, the son writes to open, expand, and explore. Beginning with as bald a declaration of facts as possible, he interprets, speculates, and generalizes. Handke challenges, where his mother accomodated, the attitudes that enclosed her in the "narrow circle," allowing no room for imagination, adventure, or experimentation. As a writer he exercises those freedoms, as though to make up for her captivity. He imagines himself into her life, tells it not just as it was, but in terms of what it might have become. The telling is a bold experiment in form, which enhances the uniqueness and importance of the life story. If in living she "became nothing," writing makes her "something"--an exemplary case--an indictment tot he complacent.

Another of her self-destructive survival strategies was to wear masks. Since individuality was punished, Handke observes, she gradually learned to extinguish her individuality and to "become a type." Imitation, pretense, and disguise were the skills she developed to "get along." She buried her particularity and assumed

> a masklike face--not rigid as a mask but with a masklike immobility--a disguised voice, which for fear of attracting attention not only spoke the foreign dialect but mimicked the foreign turns of phrase . . . a copied posture, with a bend at the hips and one foot thrust forward . . . all this in order to become, not a different person, but a type . . . (25)

She did not succeed in becoming a type. Toward the end of her life she began to care less about social judgments, began to read, and, Handke recalls, "was gradually becoming an individual," but only in time to see that it was too late--to convince her that "she could have made something of herself" (45-48ff).

In presenting his mother as a character, Handke treats her both as type and as individual. He wants to commemorate her individuality, and yet to give her life public relevance. He uses her typicality to highlight her as a character rather than submerge her, once again bringing the opposite sides of a phenomenon together to prevent either from seeming to be the whole truth. In telling the story, he continually confronts the problem of maintaining balance between the two "dangers" of over-generalizing and over-emphasizing particulars. "The danger of all these abstractions and formulations," he writes, "is of course that they tend to become independent. When that happens, the individual that gave rise to them is forgotten . . . in every sentence I am afraid of losing my balance"(29). He keeps his balance by a strategy of constant alternation, each section--sometimes each paragraph--becoming a corrective to the previous one.

If the woman herself "became a type" in order to conceal and repress or mask her individuality, the writer makes her a type in order to reveal and express something essential about her, making her typicality a backdrop to her uniqueness. The danger he wants to avoid is of making the story into "a literary ritual in which an individual life ceases to be anything more than a pretext" (28). Both aspects of her character are essential. He uses type to unmask rather than to mask.

Handke quotes a letter written shortly before his mother's death: "I can't stand it in the house any more, so I'm always gadding about somewhere" (58) . To "go outside," to escape, to distract herself, to avoid, are all efforts to stay on the periphery. She feared what was inside. Writing about her, Handke determinedly counteracts this escapism: he tries, as he puts it, to "penetrate" the surface of the life, to "go inside," to confront, to get past protective cliches. Going again and again to the inside, resisting the pull toward distracting surface detail, using detail always in the service of the larger objective, requires vigilant self-consciousness and a willingness to remain true to the moments of insight in the course of co position, adapting the narrative process at each stage as perspective shifts. Always we are brought back to the present moment, the moment of composition, the moment of remembering. The book is also about the interpenetration of past and present. As in any autobiographical work, the past is resurrected and transformed by being incorporated into the living present. This is, indeed, an essential characteristic of autobiography: the past can only be made meaningful in terms of the present moment from which it is regarded. And only by maintaining the focus on the particular and immediate truth as opposed to the general and universal can autobiography remain faithful to its own particular purpose; the individual life cannot be a basis for general truths except by being true to its own peculiarities. "If he is courageously open to the synthesizing process of meaning-making," Barrett Mandel writes,

> the autobiographer will have produced a valid, honest, and perfectly true revelation of his life, couched in and defined by his horizons. The truth of the author's *life* will doubtlessly undergo erosion or alteration if he lives on for many years, but the truth of the *book* cannot change if it has vividly and honestly illuminated the past as experienced in a moment of now.[28]

Stages in Transformation

Asked in an interview to comment upon the course of his work, Elie Wiesel replied, "*Night* was the foundation. All the rest is commentary.[29] His many fictional and dramatic works grew out of the autobiography. All elaborate upon themes introduced there, building imaginatively upon the memories that took their first literary form in that book. In a similar way, Wolf and Rich use their journals as raw material for later works. Impressions, feelings, insights registered there later become part of a larger narrative pattern. The autobiographical act is a continuing process of revision and transformation of memories through writing.

The forms of autobiography can, in fact, be seen as stages in the transformation of event into story. As a writer gains distance from an experience, his rendering of it tends to become increasingly articulated, patterned, and imaginative. At each stage in the process a different form of writing emerges. The forms autobiography progressively assumes may be characterized by the descriptive terms, "introspections," "retrospections," and "transformations." These terms categorize autobiographies according to the writer's distance in time from events recounted and the degree of reshaping involved in the tale. Each also emphasizes an aspect of translating experience into writing: the first is predominantly description; the second composition--selection, arrangement, and connection of facts; and the third elaboration. Introspections arise in the moment, such as entries in diaries or journals. They express the immediacy of the urge to record. Often they tend to be the least artful.[30] Generally the therapeutic initiative in this kind of writing dominates, particularly in a period of crisis. Lewis records that he is writing his journal in order to "get a little distance" from his grief; his main objective at the outset is to assuage pain.

A Grief Observed provides a fairly typical example of the introspective form. In four manuscript books he found "lying about the house," Lewis tried to set down "the plain facts of agonizing experience:" the shifting feelings and conflicting thoughts, the questions, outrage, and despair. The published text of his journal falls into four sections, corresponding simply to the four notebooks he filled. Yet these divisions are not just arbitrary, for each new notebook provides him with a sense of a new beginning. As he begins each one he reorients himself and reassesses his project. Each notebook represents a considered decision to continue the process.[31]

Within each section, individual entries are undated and divided simply by double spaces. Internal evidence suggests that Lewis was writing at least one entry, sometimes several, a day. Particularly in the first notebook, the entries are loosely linked fragments, though later that discontinuity gives way to more continuous development of ideas. Among the thoughts and feelings Lewis records is a gnawing ambivalence about the journal itself: "Are these jottings morbid?" he asks.

> Do these notes merely . . . confirm the monotonous, tread-mill march of the mind round one subject? But

> what am I to do? I must have some drug, and reading isn't a strong enough drug now. By writing it all down . . . I believe I get a little outside it. (10)

Lewis expresses two distinct attitudes here toward the writing process: as a "drug," it provides an analgesic, a way of dulling the pain. But the belief that writing helps him to "get outside" the pain suggests a more constructive function: writing objectifies his suffering and prevents him from drowning in it.

Lewis obviously found some value in both the process and the result, since he decided a year later to have the journal published as *A Grief Observed*, under the pseudonym of N.W. Clerk. His unprecedented use of a pseudonym and a mere initial, H., to identify his wife, indicates Lewis's persistent ambivalence about the undertaking, as did his attitude toward the work, once published. Roger Green notes, "When it came out, Lewis does not seem to have sent copies to friends, and never alluded to it."[32] The purpose of the journal was to explore the experience of grief, to examine Christian pieties in light of this bitter experience, and to speak truly about its effect upon his faith. But the urgency of that intention was undermined by fear of giving scandal. At the time he wrote and published the book, Lewis was already a Christian apologist of international reputation. His mail regularly brought letters from people all over the world seeking guidance in matters of faith. His sense of moral responsibility to those people competed with his need and desire to speak in a different voice about this dark night of the soul.

A Grief Observed reveals a side to Lewis that is carefully veiled in all his other work. It is his book of *Job*, a bitter struggle with himself and with God, in which he is at times enraged, cynical, and near despair. In it he makes a desperate effort to bring the truths he has so earnestly championed into some congruence with the radical ironies grief has forced upon him. The emotional honesty of the book makes it unique in his canon. In his earlier autobiographical narrative, *Surprised by Joy* (1952), Lewis wrote that he had, from childhood, "a certain distrust or dislike of emotion as something uncomfortable and embarrassing and even dangerous."33 This native tendency to distrust and dismiss emotions shows up in *A Grief Observed* as a fear of maudlin sentimentality, morbidity, and self-indulgence. Nevertheless, his ruthless scrutiny of those tendencies accompanies an equally determined effort to get beyond intellectual abstractions about grief and death, thus giving his emotional self a voice.

Lewis acknowledges in the journal the importance of feelings in determining how we know and what we believe. And though he concludes by reaffirming universal truths to which all particular experiences are subordinate, that reaffirmation is deeply and permanently qualified by the spiritual struggle which this journal of grief records. In his journal, an inveterate intellectual expresses powerful feelings, doubts, and questions; they take him beyond what the intellect can adequately answer. He is testing his beliefs on his nerve-ends. He sees his bereavement as a "trial by fire" which pushes him to the limit of what his faith can endure.

His faith does endure. By the end of the journal, tone and perspective have changed. The voice is no longer that of a bewildered and shattered victim, but of a resolute survivor, determined if not unshaken in his faith, who has not been defeated by grief, but can look back down that "winding valley" and begin to see with a larger view where he has been. In retrospect, grieving begins to look like a finite process. In the last pages, A Grief Observed becomes more autobiography than journal; the process of summation and assimilation and artistic recomposition have begun.

Writing an autobiography differs from journal writing in several obvious ways. Principles of selection are more defined, perspective tends to be more stable, and events are connected by continuous narrative rather than as discrete units. Memories are brought into greater coherence and assimilated into a larger matrix of experience. Retrospection generally produces more artful composition than introspection, and expands outward from description to implication. Composition becomes at this stage a more complex act, involving a careful sifting of materials and defining of values. Autobiographies generally achieve a greater balance between artistic and therapeutic concerns than journals. To call a work an autobiography raises certain generic expectations, among which are continuity, factuality, and coherence, as well as comprehensible logic.

In the act of composition a writer thus assumes control over the events he records. In this context, healing becomes a process of growing self-possession, and an author's power lies in taking possession of the events of his life and recasting them. In autobiography the transformation of events is primarily structural. The obligation to "witness" is stronger than the inclination to expand upon facts. But one often gives way to the other, once events are duly recorded. Wiesel reflects upon how this process has continued for him into a whole career of both fictive and factual writing:

> When I wrote [*Night*] in 1955, while I wrote it, it might have been the only book I would have written. To me, it would have been enough. I did what I had to do. I think, in re-reading it, I suddenly realized that to stay with the past was not enough. We must take the past and transcend it.[34]

Fictionalization is an important turning point in that process of achieving transcendence. Any autobiographer will acknowledge that narration produces fictions, but he reaches a distinctly new stage when fictions become designed and deliberate. Just as the therapeutic initiative gives way to the artistic, so also the concern for accuracy gives way to narrative demands. Fiction is no longer betrayal of the past, but creation of something with its own "life" or proper existence. As soon as that happens, as Stephen Spender has observed, "the autobiographical is transformed. It is no longer the writer's own experience: it becomes everyone's. He is no longer writing about himself: he is writing about life."[35]

What I am calling "transformations" are the many variants of autobiographical narration, carried out in a multitude of both factual and fictional forms. The impulse that governs this kind of autobiographical writing is once again complex. Fictionalization is not an escape from truth, but an attempt to tell a different kind of truth, often a larger truth, than can arise through presentation of the facts. Roy Pascal writes of two nineteenth-century authors who seemed to gravitate toward fiction out of inner necessity to tell a "real truth" about their lives:

> The actuality of their lives would have been, for [Gottfried] Keller and Charlotte Bronte, a 'wrong truth.' They know themselves to be other than they were in actuality, and obey the 'sense of life' instead of the historical facts. In so doing, they do something more. Overcoming what in their characters and circumstances they felt to be fortuitous, they also make their heroes and their novels more generally true, more illuminating about personality in general, more relevant to everyone. And in this process a curious transformation occurs that distinguishes art.36

At the stage of autobiographical process described here, the artistic initiative has overtaken the therapeutic. Fictionalization implies a certain detachment from one's own experience--or an understanding of its implications that goes deeper than presented facts and may even demand alteration of those facts in order to be truly expressed.

The poles of the spectrum posited here define a trajectory that describes the healing process fairly consistently. We can see that the motivation behind all autobiographical acts falls somewhere between the therapeutic and the artistic; between inward and outward focus; between formlessness and crafted form; between description and invention. The writing produced at each stage in the emergence of the self-created self has its own peculiar values and invokes different criteria for readers. At each stage something falls away. Hence, many autobiographers quote rather than paraphrase their own journals. They can never again write about the event with quite the same immediacy, nor recapture the "raw experience," except as readers of their own accounts of it.

Perhaps the most important differentiating factor among the forms of autobiography distinguished here is the degree of authority assumed by the writer. Some writers, when they record critical experiences in their journals, see themselves as vehicles or victims of circumstance. Writing for them is a recording of external events as presented from the outside. But as the writer "takes possession" of the event, he acquires authority and increasingly presents himself as agent rather than victim--one who shapes and defines circumstances rather than simply suffering them.

Sometimes the process of moving through these stages of autobiographical composition can result in coming full circle: in recent years many women writers have chosen deliberately to tell their stories in the somewhat fragmented and shifting style of journal writing in order to recreate the immediacy and spontaneity that might be lost in more conventional narration. But such texts are also a result of craftsmanship, as surely as the primitive paintings that look like the work of children, but far from naive, project what Adrienne Rich calls "hard-won simplicity."

Narrative Structures: Linear, Circular, Simultaneous

"I will begin, then . . ." Peter Handke writes on the sixth page of *A Sorrow Beyond Dreams*. At that point he begins the narrative of his mother's life, his means of searching for the roots of her despair. The actual beginning of the book is his mother's obituary. The book begins with an ending, and is a search for beginnings.

When he is working with clients in writing therapy, Ira Progoff has them divide their lives into periods and keep what he calls a "period log." A "period" is defined as any segment of life that seems to have a definite beginning and end. The object in therapy is to gain a sense of orientation, to assess the roots and effects of change, and to provide perspective. Interestingly, Progoff also claims that if a person were to perform the same exercise each year, dividing his life into identifiable periods or chapters, the divisions would be different each time, due to changed vantage points. Beginnings and endings are relative.

Christa Wolf asks, When did it begin? How did we become what we are? What are the roots of change? To draw perimeters around a period of crisis is the beginning of authorial control. Finding a beginning is a structuring act, for there are no absolute beginnings--only markers in the continuum of life that we agree to designate as beginnings.

James Cox discusses the problem of beginnings and endings in his essay, "Autobiography and America," defining autobiography as essentially historical narrative with fictive aspects:

> There is . . . striking difference between the nature of historical and fictive narrative. In historical narrative the beginning and the ending are by necessity arbitrary and unreal (perhaps untrue would be the better term), for history has no beginning and no end. Thus the historian has to set up a principle of organization which will justify a beginning and an ending, concealing his intrusion into the irreversible historical stream. . . . His exit and entrance are the two sure fictive aspects of his form.[37]

Beginning and ending a story of crisis objectifies the experience, transforms the victim-self into a character and separates that self from the author-self who shapes and controls the telling. While one may look back at a "crisis period" and pronounce it ended, it is more difficult to say when healing is complete. Defining the "end" is important, however, just as a decision to terminate therapy is important: it is the act by which the individual asserts that healing has occurred, that the crisis is past, that he has found a new balance, however delicate it may still be.

Lewis's decision to stop writing out his grief came not from having reached a resounding conclusion, but from recognizing that the process could go on indefinitely. He made this decision upon beginning the last of his four notebooks: "I resolve to let this limit my jottings. I will not start buying books for the purpose. . . . if I don't stop writing . . . at some quite arbitrary point, there's no reason why I should ever stop. There is something new to be chronicled every day. (68-69) At no point can one say with finality, "Now I am finished with that experience." But one can write a concluding paragraph and put down the pen, and that act in itself can make an ending to a life period as well as to the text.

Like Lewis, Peter Handke realized that "grief is a long valley"--that the completion of the text is not a termination of grief. His mother's story told, he still had to find a way to continue life. The last pages of *A Sorrow Beyond Dreams* underscore the sense of incompletion and inconclusiveness with which he draws his writing to a close. The story is told, but it does not come to a comfortable closure. Suicide is a termination, not a completion. It leaves ragged edges. So does the narrative: the pages that follow Handke's account of the suicide present an apparently random collection of memories that never found their way into the story--telling details that make clear how much of the story remains untold. These postscripts remind the reader the, though the narrative may have a superficial completeness, it is artificially shaped out of a chaos of memories. As narrative form gives way to a patchwork of disconnected memories, the idea of narration itself comes into question. The story has been told, but so much clearly remains unaccounted for that the reader must qualify his sense of what the account is: not a "true" presentation of life, but a mere cross-section.

Handke also questions the healing he had supposed writing would accomplish. He has done what he meant to do when he began writing, and, as Lewis said of his own "grief work," it has prevented collapse. But, again like Lewis, Handke continues to experience new waves of grief. He opens one entry, a few pages from the end,

> It is not true that writing has helped me. in my weeks of preoccupation with the story, the story has not ceased to preoccupy me. Writing has not, as I first supposed, been a remembering of a concluded period in my life, but merely a constant pretense at remembering, in the form of sentences that only lay claim to detachment. (66)

He wonders whether he really has penetrated the surface, or whether he has succeeded only in creating an impression of depth. He hasn't overcome grief by writing it out; he wonders, in fact, whether the only cure that writing affords is temporary relief of symptoms--an illusion of healing:

> Obviously narration is only an act of memory; on the other hand, it holds nothing in reserve for future use; it merely derives a little pleasure from states of dread by trying to formulate them as aptly as possible; from enjoyment of horror it produces enjoyment of memory. (67)

Handke realizes, as he closes his book, how utterly remote the symbolic act of restoration is from the reality that cannot be restored. His mother is gone. She has, literally, "become nothing," and the resurgence of this stark reality mocks the hope with which he embarked upon his "exemplary case history:"

> Horror is something perfectly natural: the mind's horror vacui. A thought is taking shape, then suddenly it notices that there is nothing more to think. Whereupon it crashes to the ground like a figure in a comic strip who suddenly realizes that he has been walking on air. (70)

He has traced a path to nothingness with his words. All his care for precision and balance begin to seem pointless in such a moment.

Yet the final sentence of the text is another turning. It may be true that writing has not healed him; possibly it has only deepened the horror of suicide. But writing has fulfilled a need, and he needs to continue. Writing is still a way *through* grief. He needed tow rite to emerge from the first stages of a crisis. Though he reaches no conclusions, Handke's final sentence is itself a resolution, like Lewis's to "get on with it:"

"Someday I shall write about all this in greater detail" (70). This conclusion is both a promise and an acknowledgement that though real conclusions are impossible, one can and must invent them.

Writing in a well-established Jewish tradition, Wiesel acknowledges the contingency of beginnings and endings by reminding himself in each book of an underlying continuity:

> I always smuggle into every book one sentence which is the substance of the next book--a Jewish tradition. When we finish reading the Torah on Simchat Torah, we must begin again the same Torah at the same session. Because we never finish, we never begin. . . it's a continuous process.[38]

In his various works, Wiesel retraces again and again the familiar ground of his life, beginning at different places and working outward. Yet in the autobiography, *Night*, beginning and ending are well defined: the story moves from ghettoization to liberation--the parameters of events are repeatedly stretched beyond the lives of the witnesses, backward to Biblical origins, forward to succeeding generations. And events seem to radiate out in all directions. Each anecdote in the book is a self-contained story that introduces multiple possibilities of meaning. Linear discourse limits the degree to which those possibilities may be explored. To escape those limitations other modes of narration have to be employed.

Autobiography is necessarily inconclusive. As James Olney has pointed out, "In effect, the narrative is never finished, nor ever can be, within the covers of a book. . . . Furthermore, by its very nature the self is (like the autobiography that records and creates it) open-ended and incomplete: it is always in process or, more precisely, it is itself a process.[39]

Yet most narratives attempt to achieve a neatness, clarity of pattern, and closure that life itself does not have. Their artificiality in this respect is a therapeutic necessity. Two archetypal narrative patterns are the linear (a story has a beginning, middle, and end) and the circular ("In my end is my beginning.") We cannot completely separate these two, nor escape them, only note that they are but two ways of describing experience. Both tend to leave out marginal experience. The almost universal concern with the nature of time in modern narratives testifies to the extent of the problem. Chronological time is deceptive. The idea of one-directional, linear time is, as the modernists reaffirmed, a convention, not an absolute, and blinds us to some basic truths about how we live and have our being in the world.

The Aristotelian idea of "beginning, middle, and end" as the natural defining characteristic of a story line breaks down when an author perceives events as continually shifting and reshaping themselves. The past is not fixed, but always subject to revision in light of the changing present. Particularly in a period of crisis, neat linear descriptions of events prove inaccurate, since everything seems to change in a moment of new vision. When "things fall apart" it is hard to say in what order they did so, or to trace a line of causality. Causes and effects are so multiple that the terms become very nearly useless.

The idea of cyclical time, and the concomitant circular mode of narration, are correctives to linearity, because they emphasize the pervasiveness of repetition and analogy. Largely in reaction to the extremely linear world view prevalent in the nineteenth century myths of progress, early twentieth century writers such as Yeats, Joyce, and Eliot experimented with cyclical theories of history and of life cycles in their major works. Cyclical theories account for a number of aspects of life that linear theories fail to explain. They express an aesthetic ideal of condensation, for a circle is an enclosure. Shifts and changes within it remain confined to a matrix that is eternal and unchanging, suggesting, as Eliot puts it, that "all is always now"--and change is repetition with a difference. Yeats' theory of gyres and Pound's idea of the "vortex" are two more variations on the idea of circularity. In both, circularity becomes a dynamic principle, not just a geometric metaphor. Both writers play upon the ways circles form in nature: the tendency of things to find a center and constellate themselves in relation to it. It is easy to see how such observations about natural patterns lead to narrative theories.

Post-World War I writers were drawn to cyclical theories of history because so much had been destroyed. The idea that civilization might be circling back to its origins was potentially very comforting in the face of massive destruction. They also embraced cyclical theories of individual life, perhaps because their own had been, as Brittain expressed it, "smashed up," and recovery seemed like beginning again at a starting point.

Patricia Spacks has commented upon the particular prevalence of cyclical patterns in the life stories of women. She suggests that circularity is a peculiarly female mode of perception, possibly because of the repetitive nature of female life in Western culture: "In their form, women's lives tend to be like the stories that they tell: they show less a pattern of linear development towards some clear goal than one of repetitive, cumulative, cyclical structure. One thinks of housework or child care, of domestic life in general."[40] "The very concept of the life cycle," Spacks suggests, "and the successive psychological crises out of which a mature identity emerges, is a 'necessary fiction.'" Brittain's narrative traces a large circle, but with the clear message that the circle is not an entirely closed pattern: the losses are real, and beyond recovery, and, as Ezrahi later says of the Holocaust, some things are beyond analogy. Still, as she concludes with the words, "this new beginning," Brittain comes back to herself; the theme of return is strong and hopeful at the end.

Wolf, like Brittain, uses a circular form, but ironizes it. Coming back home is not a climax or triumph, merely a practical necessity. She must return to the present and the ordinary, out of liminal time. She must change from rememberer to writer if the book is to be written.

The appeal of the cyclical pattern is obvious: it suggests closure, resolution, completion, healing. When Jung diagnosed mentally disturbed patients, he sometimes handed them an unfinished figure to see if they would close it. Closing the figure was considered a normal, or healthy, response. Leaving it open he read as a sign of disturbance. The desire for closure is a deeply ingrained self-protective device. Even when we know it to be somewhat artificial, we seek a satisfying conclusion to our stories that will make them "come out right." The idea of the cycle offers security because through it the unfamiliar can be made familiar: we can say to ourselves, we have been this way before. Everything becomes analogy--repetition with a difference. And we always seem to be telling the same stories, variations on the great human themes.

But are we really? When the life stories no longer seem to fit the mythic patterns, the way we tell them has to change. To tell "the thing itself and not the myth" demands that we escape from simpler narrative modes and find truer, if more complex, ones. Re-vision means re-formation. Where both linearity and circularity fail, modern writers have attempted to invent narrative devices that reflect another dimension of existence. The line is a one-dimensional figure, the circle two-dimensional. What modern writers seem to be seeking is a "three-dimensional" mode of narration that reflects the complexity of consciousness and brings inner and outer worlds together. Both linear and circular narrative patterns are two-dimensional, and fairly simple models of reality. If progress is a myth, so are closure and repetition. A closed circle, like the Aristotelian climax, is an artificial construct. Yet closure of some kind is necessary to sanity. What happens when events neither come to closure nor reveal a clear meaning? We need to find a way to make sense of them. Existentialism has suggested one means of doing so with its emphasis on the self-contained moment, in which meaning inheres only by attribution--the authorial act of making meaning by projecting it upon a situation that is only potentially meaningful.

One writerly strategy for achieving a different kind of sense-making structure is the kind of dichotomy and dialogue that Handke, Rich, and Pirsig all use in their various ways. Each separates the narrative into two separate strands. By intertwining them, they suggest the kind of interplay that continually goes between inner and outer worlds, past and present, individual and community. Each strand represents a level of existence at which part of the story can be told. Alternation approximates the simultaneity they seek to express.

The idea of "the presence of the past" is achieved in Wolf's autobiography by her focus upon memory as the locus where things always converge. Her reflections upon the past are really reflections upon the nature and function of memory, and upon herself at present, as she writes. The kind of self-consciousness that informs *A Model Childhood* suggests over and over again that "all is always now." We are always in the moment of remembering, even as we see what is present.

Even in a narrative like Wiesel's *Night*, which seems to tell a linear, chronological story, we see the disintegration of the causal connections that usually make a linear narrative cohere. The narration is structured rather upon a series of constellating images, around which stories form themselves. (Does memory favor anecdotes? Wolf asks. Here it seems to.) One thing does not "lead to another," but events are connected by something larger and more complex than simple cause and effect. As this was true in the camps, so it is true in the narrative and so, one may infer, in the world as a whole.

Jung's notion of synchronicity provides one model of an "acausal connecting principle" that might serve to describe much modern narrative. According to this theory of how events are connected, cause and effect are often a *post hoc* imposition upon events which are really connected by a kind of convergence that might be expressed in the Biblical phrase, "in the fullness of time." Connections among events and lives are much more subtle than we tend ordinarily to assume. If we wish to explain, therefore, how things happened--particularly if those things are the world-shattering moments that come upon us in crisis, when everything seems to "fall on top of us at once"--we need a manner of telling and a principle of explanation that is correspondingly complex.

The Romantics were already involved in seeking subtler and more complex modes of narration when they began to evolve the idea of "organic form."[41] Modern narration is in the process of taking that idea a step further. And autobiographers are at the forefront of that effort, since life itself has become complex enough to demand new ways of being turned into story.

Organic Form and Dissipative Structures

Midway through her autobiography, Christa Wolf pauses to consider the problems of narrative, calling to the reader's attention the fact that he is reading a distortion of the experiences themselves:

> Ideally, the structure of the experience coincides with the structure of the narrative. . . . But there is no technique that permits translating the incredibly tangled mesh, whose threads are interlaced according to the strictest laws, into linear narrative without doing it serious damage. To speak about superimposed layers--"narrative levels"--means shifting into inexact nomenclature and falsifying the real process. "Life," the real process, is always steps ahead; to catch it at its latest phase remains an unsatisfiable, perhaps an impermissible desire. (272)

Form itself is a "necessary fiction." We cannot see life in its totality and present a faithful picture of that any more than we can see the entire surface of a sphere at once. One way of compensating is to create an illusion of wholeness. Another is, like Wolf, to deliberately dispel that illusion, qualifying the narrative continually to produce an "alienation effect" in the reader, warning him against presuming that he knows the whole truth of the story he is reading. She is deconstructive while at the same time maintaining an ideal of holistic discourse.

In his work on the "Intensive Journal," Progoff was searching for "an instrument that was capable of drawing together the multiplicity of contents of a human life, compressing them into a manageable space while not losing the quality of movement and change that is their essence."[42] A similar objective lies behind the experiments in organic form undertaken by the modern autobiographers we have been discussing: to express in a language and syntax that are inescapably linear something of the multi-levelled, simultaneous, dynamic and synchronous quality of the events of inner life.

William Howarth has explained the idea of organic form as the conviction that "Meaning is not imposed upon facts, it emerges from them--slowly, organically, as the ideas and images seem to find each other."[43] This description of the process reveals several distinctively modern assumptions about the process of composition: that it is partly non-rational and receptive, that it requires attentiveness at each moment to a constellation of events and ideas that are emerging and changing, and that the author must provide a locus where these things can happen--a "zone of consciousness." Metpahors of writing have changed fundamentally in this post-Romantic era, away from mechanistic concepts toward organic ones, and the corresponding image of the writer's task has resulted in a very different, more inclusive idea of authorship.

The notion of organic form implies that an author in the process of composition, like a woman during gestation, must "allow" something to happen within him as much as he "strives" to make it happen. Jung, and later Progoff, explained this process as the natural action of symbols. Symbols have a dynamic, living quality that tends to order one's life and perceptions around them. In the act of composition a symbol can become not only the coefficient of an idea, but an organizing principle. Writing is a process of the flowering out of symbols from the seeds of ideas. Form may be implicit but not preconceived--arising dialectically from conscious and unconscious sources, a dialogue between the writer and his developing text, rather than a fixed structure into which the ideas and images are fitted.

Wiesel writes about the process he undergoes when he begins a work of fiction:

> I only know the first page and the melody. If the melody is there, what we call in Hasidism the ***nigun***, the chant, is there, then it works. If not, I don't begin the novel and I go to the other side of my work, the non-fiction, the research and Talmud, Bible, Hasidism and I wait until the melody will come.[44]

Wiesel's description resembles Rich's explanation of her poetry-making process. When she writes that her poems no longer describe, but *are* experiences, she is talking about a similar attitude of receptivity to the fluctuations of consciousness that make composition an organic act.[45]

These notions of composition and form relate to and perhaps derive from similar concepts that have arisen in all other areas of thought. Aesthetic and formal questions are ultimately inseparable from ethical and epistemological ones. A writer translates philosophical problems into problems of narrative when he writes. In their efforts to find ways to "write whole," writers are pursuing a quest analogous to the physicists' search for a unified field theory.

Truth cannot be told wholly and definitively, for ambiguity lies at the heart of reality; rationality is only one aspect of consciousness. What we need to account for is the quality of unboundedness, open-endedness, and continual change that characterizes nature. It is not nouns, but verbs that locate us in the world. We are beginning to look more at the how than at the what of things. In 1910 Edwin Shuman, a literary critic, wrote, "Content is more important than form."[46] Few critics would endorse that belief now, or even the dichotomy upon which is is so soundly predicated, recognizing that the values embodied in most literary works inhere in their form as much as in their ideas.

One scientific concept articulated as recently as 1977 offers a way of understanding some modern experiments in form. In that year a Belgian physicist, Ilya Prigogine, won the Nobel Prize for his theory of "dissipative structures." The theory attempts to bridge the gap between biology and physics by exploring the oxymoronic idea of dynamic structure. Observing that forms in nature are generally open systems, continually changing within the larger patterns that allow us to perceive them as stable, he questions the idea of stability, suggesting rather that instability is the key to understanding structure. "Instability," he claims, "is the key to transformation. . . . The elements of the pattern come into contact with each other in new ways and make new connections. The parts reorganize into a new whole. The system escapes into a higher order."[47]

This idea has a number of fascinating applications to narrative theory. Perhaps Eliot anticipated something like it when he wrote the line in *Four Quartets* : "And do not call it fixity, where past and future are gathered." A text--particularly an autobiographical text--is a "gathering place" for past and future. Ideally it is not fixed, but changes as interpretive horizons change. Such a text is thus a dissipative structure, continually open to and capable of sustaining changing interpretations, while retaining its own integrity. Like the physical structures Prigogine describes, a text keeps disintegrating and reintegrating according to new and "higher" principles invested in it by readers. It is an open vessel, capable of being filled again and again, whose shape may even change, but not its quality of life.

If the art of autobiography may be taken as an index of changing consciousness, one of the things it indicates is a movement toward more complex consciousness. *A Model Childhood* offers one example of "dissipative structure" in a literary work. In it the breakdown of memories and storytelling conventions--what appears at times almost to be a disintegration of narrative--leads to reorganization at a higher level. The disjunctive finally becomes constructive, an effort to unify the disparate levels of consciousness and narration into a single act of memory and communication.

Finally the essential requisite of a literary form is that it make experience accessible; that it allow for communion between author and audience. Higher consciousness would lead to isolation if it could not be made accessible and shared. Literary forms make us aware not only of how things happen, but of who we are--what it is that forms the basis of our common humanity. The deep structures of our thought and language unite us, and if we are to be healed by the process of finding and using forms, that healing cannot take place in isolation, but must come from an effort, which literature represents, to forge connections between our various lives.

---

1 J. McConnell, *The Shattered Self: The Psychological and Religious Search for Selfhood* (Philadelphia: Pilgrim Press, 1971), p. 99.

2 McConnell, p. 99.

[3] Robert Sayre, "The Proper Study: Autobiographies in American Studies" in *The American Autobiography*, ed., Albert E. Stone (Englewood Cliffs, NJ: Prentice-Hall, 1981), p. 19.

[4] Adrienne Rich, "The Insomniacs" in *Poems: Selected and New*, 1950-1974 (New York: W.W. Norton and Co., 1975), p. 28.

[5] See, for instance, her essay, "When We Dead Awaken" in Gelpi, pp. 90-98.

[6] Rich, "The Roofwalkers," in Gelpi, p. 20.

[7] Gunn, pp. 25-26.

[8] Susan Friedman, "Theories of Autobiography and Modernist Self-Creations in H.D.'s Canon." Paper presented at the 1983 convention of the Modern Language Association, New York, p. 1.

[9] Spengemann, Introduction.

[10] William Empson, Some Versions of Pastoral (Norfolk, CN: New Directions Books, 1960), p. 23.

[11] Francis Hart, "Notes for an Anatomy of Modern Autobiography," *New Literary History* 1 (1970) 485-511.

[12] Alfred Kazin in Stone, p. 42.

[13] Elizabeth Bruss, *Autobiographical Acts: The Changing Situation of a Literary Genre* (Baltimore: Johns Hopkins University Press, 1976), p. 90.

[14] Ezrahi, pp. 3-4.

[15] William L. Howarth, "Some Principles of Autobiography," in Olney, p. 88.

[16] Stephen Spender, "Confessions and Autobiography" in Olney, p. 117.

17 Hayden White, "The Value of Narrativity," in W.J.T. Mitchell, *On Narrative* (Chicago: University of Chicago Press, 1981), pp. 2-3.

18 Gusdorf, "Conditions and Limits" in Olney, p. 37.

19 Robert Scholes, "Language, Narrative and Anti-Narrative" in Mitchell, p. 208.

20 Cargas, p. 96.

21 Cargas, p. 110.

22 Cargas, p. 25.

23 Ezrahi, p. 119.

24 Ezrahi, p. 117.

25 Lawrence Langer, *Versions of Survival: The Holocaust and the Human Spirit* (Albany: State University of New York Press, 1982), p. x.

26 Langer, pp. 17-18.

27 Ezrahi, p. 4.

28 Barrett Mandel, "Full of Life Now," in Olney, p. 70.

29 Cargas, p. 3.

30 Poetry, of course, often written in times of extreme crisis, may be a counter-example to this theory, but does not, I think, discount it.

31 See, for example, opening remarks at the beginning of the third section.

[32] Roger Green and Walter Hooper, *C.S. Lewis: A Biography* (New York: Harcourt, Brace, Jovanovich, 1974), p. 277.

[33] C.S. Lewis, *Surprised by Joy: The Shape of My Early Life* (New York: Harcourt, Brace and Co., 1955), pp. 11-12.

[34] Cargas, p. 89.

[35] Spender, p. 117.

[36] Pascal, p. 168.

[37] James Cox, "Autobiography and America," *Virginia Quarterly Review* 47 (1971) 252-277.

[38] Cargas, p. 91.

[39] Olney, p. 25.

[40] Spacks, p. 33.

[41] M.H. Abrams dates the concept of organic form from the early nineteenth century when writers began to use organic processes and natural forms as metaphors for literary activity.

[42] Progoff, *Journal* , p. 21.

[43] Howarth, p. 111.

[44] Cargas, p. 94.

[45] Adrienne Rich, "Poetry and Experience: Statement at a Poetry Reading in 1964" in Gelpi, p. 89.

[46] Edwin Shuman, *How to Judge a Book: A Handy Method of Criticism for the General Reader* (New York: Houghton, Mifflin Co., 1910), p. 20.

[47] Marilyn Ferguson, *The Aquarian Conspiracy: Personal and Social Transformation in the 1980's* (Los Angeles: J.P. Tarcher, Inc., 1980), pp. 164-165.

CHAPTER 6

BEING ALONE AND BEING CONNECTED

Crisis and Isolation

One of the darkest moments Christa Wolf describes in *A Model Childhood* is an experience of complete spiritual isolation:

> Desperation was not the proper expression for it, because, to be able to despair, indicates a connection with the cause of the desperation. Nelly was no longer connected with anything. . . . Since all outside commands had broken down, she had to adhere even more strictly to something within, which perhaps prevented her from going stark raving mad on the spot. (267)

Wolf is describing an experience commonly recalled by victims of crisis. The sense that the world has failed them drives them inward for some principle of coherence: at least in the recesses of their own minds they may manufacture a consistent frame of reference, and an environment that can be ordered and controlled. Yet thought that "strict adherence to something within" may prevent madness for a time, it is also the beginning of madness.

Healing cannot take place in such isolation. We do not live alone, and were not meant to. Reconnection completes the healing process. In her study of the writings of concentration camp victims, Sidra Ezrahi comments upon the survival value of human connections: "Preservation of the spirit as well as the body is far more likely where the individual remains attached to a mutually sustaining group, even if the group comprises only one other person."[1] The other serves as a mirror, a counterbalance, a reality check. As we have seen, healing often takes place through dialogue, because dialogue prevents wither solipsistic self-absorption or self-abandonment.

A time of relative seclusion in a period of crisis may be necessary for gathering spiritual forces, sifting values, eliminating things that confuse and debilitate; but if healing means wholeness, then eventually that retreat into the depths of the self must lead back into community because we are not complete in ourselves, but parts of a larger whole. Albert Gelpi describes Rich's recovery from a long period of crisis as a "re-entry" into communal life:

> For Rich . . . a deepening subjectivity does not mean withdrawal, as it did for Dickinson, but, on the contrary, a more searching engagement with people and with social forces. 'Necessities of Life,' the first poem in [the volume of that title], notes her re-entry into the world after a time of guarded isolation.[2]

Ideally, the "deepening subjectivity" Gelpi speaks of produces a deeper capacity for empathy. Only a person who has plumbed his own depths can enter into other lives with real understanding. For Rich, poetry is the means of connection. She touches other lives by making her own inner life accessible, serving as that mirror or touchstone for others. Like Anais Nin, Rich believes that "the personal life deeply lived" can be the deepest kind of participation in common life.

Literature is an ongoing dialogue that con sustain our shared life by providing a common ground of reference. It serves not only as a means of self-expression for the writer, but by providing a common language connects writer with reader and brings readers into community, providing the touchstones they share. Literature is not simply an ornament to social intercourse, but a spiritual necessity. There is a sacramental aspect to the literary enterprise that, like the sacrament of communion, creates a field of shared consciousness, and reinforces recognition of what we have in common as human beings.

Merleau-Ponty claims that forging these bonds of recognition is one of the essential functions of art. "It is not enough," he writes, "for a painter like Cezanne, an artist, or a philosopher, to create and express an idea; they must also awaken the experience which will make their idea take root in the consciousness of others."3 In other words, the task of the writer is not only to inform, but to awaken. An idea that "takes root" in another's consciousness will be one he comes to understand and experience as though it originated with him; it will become his own. This is what shared life means: when one reads an autobiography, something of that life becomes a part of his own as he reads and recognizes and responds with the "Me, too!" that is somehow deeply reassuring.

By definition an autobiographer is endeavoring to connect with others at that deep level of shared humanity--to find in his or her own life story where the unique meets the universal. Perhaps only those who have been driven into radical isolation are capable of the deepest kind of connection: at the bottom of the well they reach the underground stream that is the common source. Wiesel has experienced the extremes of isolation and still cherishes solitude, yet his writing builds bridges to other lives and places him in the midst of an ever-widening community. He sees his vocation as a continual balancing of solitude and interaction: "The creative process . . . comes from solitude, it goes to solitude, and yet it's a meeting between two solitudes. . . . when you write and someone reads you . . . your solitude is faced with the reader's and you join with that solitude."4 The quality of intimacy in the relationship between writer and reader described here recalls Rilke's ideal of love as a free meeting of two single and separate souls: ". . . two solitudes [that] protect and border and salute each other."5

Strangely, those things we have most in common, like suffering, separate us even as they connect us. Suffering is the common lot of humanity, but, as Lewis came to realize while sitting at his wife's bedside, we cannot really share the suffering even of those to whom we are most deeply connected, except in a vicarious way. "You can't really share someone else's weakness, or fear or pain," he writes. "What you feel may be bad . . . but it would still be quite different" (13). Words, however, make bridges between our islands. Communication can quite literally be communion. While it may not dispel suffering, it can take the sting of loneliness out of it.

In Wolf's and Pirsig's autobiographies we see the hope that communication will prevent repetition of suffering. What they tell their children--and by extension their readers--is in part a warning and a shield against the forces that once drove them respectively into isolation and insanity. They see themselves as representative members of one generation trying to make their memories accessible and useful to the next, contributing to the cultural memory that is our only protection against "history's grievous repetitions." Wolf reflects ruefully on how difficult that sharing is, however--how much estranges her from her own child, how quickly the language of her own generation has faded into obsolescence, how delicately one must search for a common language that will prevent the formulations of historians from obliterating acutal experience. She reflects upon her daughter's reactions to stories of the war years:

> (Lenka says that this is what she can imagine least of all: to be faced with one's own death night after night. This may be the ultimate generation gap: the experience that one can be threatened with death and still not die, not commit crimes, not go mad.) (303-4)

The child must know what can be endured and survived, if only to provide a standard for her still naive convictions about what can and ought to be. And the message is there for any reader: we are members of one species, more like one another than different. We seek relief from isolation not only for our own comfort, but because, in the end, we should ideally be able to look at the broad spectrum of lives and say with true sympathy, "Nothing human is alien to me."

My Story, Our Story: Individual and Communal Identity

Vera Brittain left her private desk and diary to travel around the world speaking for the League of Nations. Adrienne Rich continues an odyssey that began in private journals and poetry on public podiums, working for more enlightened community among women. Elie Wiesel tours the country every year, seeking to unite the Jewish community and, beyond them, all people in a shared understanding of the implications of the Holocaust for our time. The writing that helped each of these authors emerge from personal crises has also deepened their sense of social responsibility. And their writings have become their means of fulfilling that responsibility. In a recent interview, Wiesel explained his understanding of the role of a writer in the community:

> Let's take the problem of suffering because it's one of the elements that moves me to write. If someone suffers and he keeps silent, it can be a good silence. If someone suffers and I keep silent, then it's a destructive silence. If we envisage literature and human destiny as endeavors by man to redeem himself, then we must admit the obsession, the overall dominating theme of responsibility, that we are responsible for one another.[6]

This view of the writer's vocation implies a paradox: he must stand apart from the community to gain perspective upon it, yet also deeply identify himself with the community in which he lives, with a fineness of social conscience that approaches the ideal Lewis articulates in reflecting upon his own grief: "If I had really cared, as I thought I did, about the sorrows of the world, I should not have been so overwhelmed when my own sorrow came" (42).

If literature is, as Wiesel sees it, a "redemptive" act, the writer must in some sense be a redeemer, one who lives out the life of the community in full measure, being in it, but not of it. In this capacity, Wiesel says "When I say 'I,' I speak as a Jew because I am Jewish and I assume the entire destiny of my people from beginning to now. As a Jew I believe that to be a Jew is to be an opening. But when the Jew is Jewish he speaks on behalf of everybody."[7] The religious model implied here is not uncommon, particularly among autobiographers who have chosen to offer up their lives to be consumed by others, making themselves into standards by which others can measure their own experience.

Wiesel identifies his position in the Jewish community as "witness from within and defender from without." "This goes, of course," he adds, "along with my ideas about the duties and privileges of a storyteller--of a writer."[8] One of those privileges is to be able to say, as he does, "He who says I says I for all men."[9] But the privilege carries a cost: the writer who thus makes his own life an example makes himself vulnerable to public judgment. The author takes a great risk, Wiesel comments, in "stripping himself to give us the truth." He becomes terribly vulnerable:

> What he does, he understands, will have to be inadequate. We may, if we wish, laugh at his nakedness. He must have what Alfred Adler called, 'the courage of imperfection.' This courage exists in an artist's willingness to make a mistake as he searches for truth, comprehending that from his mistakes he and others can learn more truth.[10]

Autobiography might seem by definition a solitary act. Focused as it is upon the individual life, it would seem to have far less to do with political and social realities than other forms of history. Janet Varner Gunn believes that the danger of solipsism inheres in the autobiographical act.[11] That danger can only be averted by a humility that sees beyond the particulars of individual life and recognizes our fundamental interdependence. This recognition must survive even in the midst of the most personal memories and private thoughts. The writer only becomes a "redeemer" if he or she is first completely engaged in working out his or her own salvation. He or she only becomes a representative voice by being true to his own individuality. George Steiner comments on his account of himself and his Jewish origins,

> This is my self-definition. Mine, because I cannot speak for any other Jew. All of us obviously have something in common. We do tend to recognize one another wherever we meet, nearly at a glance, by some common trick of feeling, by the darkness we carry. But each of us must hammer it out for himself.[12]

Each of the autobiographies examined here is predicated upon the conviction that individual healing or enlightenment will resonate in a larger sphere--that the healing of an individual life can help to bring about healing in the community. Foucault's claim that a work of literature is an expression of collective consciousness is as true of autobiography as of any other literary form--perhaps even more so.[13] Moreover, the best writers not only articulate the collective consciousness, but also bring to light that faculty which Jung claims is "common to all . . . the foundation of what the ancients call 'the sympathy of all things.'"[14]

The autobiographer is not by any means "above" or apart from the influences he or she brings to consciousness. On the contrary, he is deeply affected by the community from which he emerges. As Peter Berger says,

> The world encompasses the biography of the individual, which unfolds as a series of events within that world. . . the individual's own life appears as objectively real, to himself as well as to others, only as it is located within a social world that itself has the character of objective reality.[15]

Even the most private aspects of the autobiographical act take place in silent dialogue with the community, though the dialectical process may remain submerged in the narrative. Janet Varner Gunn observes that

> The reading of oneself is always a cultural reading since self-knowledge, far from being transcendent or free-floating, is always grounded in the signs of one's existence that are received from others, as well as from the works of culture by which one is interpreted.[16]

If the danger of solipsism attends the autobiographical act on the one side, the danger of betraying one's own insights through subordination to communal consciousness lies on the other side of that narrow path of self-expression. Estelle Jelinek finds in women's autobiographies a strong tendency to subordinate individual to communal consciousness:

> as we examine these spiritual autobiographies . . . a telling pattern emerges. The women mirror the community's standards and the community's struggles. In its broadest outlines, it is not the individual's voice that we hear but rather that of the community manifested through the peculiar stamp of the individual woman.[17]

This tendency is a strength insofar as cooperation and bonding create a strong social fabric and enhance people's lives. But while this style of autobiography serves the important function of articulating shared life, it also reveals how easily the self can get lost in collectivity. Patricia Spacks describes some of the more destructive or dangerous ways in which this relationship of autobiographer to community has worked in the past for women:

> The very fact that women so often describe themselves in the terms men might use to describe them suggests that their ways of writing, like their ways of living, frequently represent attempts to conquer by *incorporating* the damaging stereotypes of society.[18]

The autobiographer's problem, then, is one of balance: to maintain intact the contours of his or her own unique life story while making it a mirror for other lives as well.

Identity and Change: Individuals and Institutions

If at one level the function of autobiography is religious--if, as Ezrahi claims, it is a ritual of meaning that "replaces our disrupted ceremonies,"[19] perhaps it has assumed that function in response to a need engendered by the disintegration of religious institutions. Peter Berger claims that we cannot exist apart from institutions that give us identity and meaning, even though they are fallible products of human consciousness. As we objectify and sacralize them, they act back upon us. "Every individual biography," he writes,

> is an episode within the history of society, which both precedes and survives it. . . . it is within society, and as a result of social processes, that the individual becomes a person, that he attains and holds onto an identity, and

> that he carries out the various projects that constitute his life.[20]

Crisis often comes from the discrepancies between lived experience and the expectations fostered by institutions that provide us with identity. If, as Berger claims, "the cosmization of . . . institutions permits the individual to have an ultimate sense of rightness, both cognitively and normatively, in the roles he is expected to play in society,"[21] separation from those institutions leaves the individual on very shaky ground. Yet institutions that have been our support structures can sometimes turn into prisons. A crisis of faith expresses the failure of individual life to bear out definitions and prescriptions of an institution. This is most obvious in the case of religious crises such as those described by Lewis and Wiesel. Both men struggle to maintain their respective identities as Christian and Jew by carefully reexamining the obligations and definitions those labels impose upon them. In writing their own stories they redefine their traditions in the light of personal experience.

The dialectical struggle between individual experience and institutionalized identity becomes explicit in Adrienne Rich's *Of Woman Born*. Her subtitle, "Motherhood as Experience and Institution," introduces that polarization as an overarching theme. Her problem is possibly more acute than the "crises of faith" Lewis and Wiesel describe, because motherhood is not commonly understood as a formal institution, but only a loose body of expectations now entrenched in our society.

What happens when an institution becomes a prison? One's relationship with it becomes antagonistic. The authority of one's own perceptions and desires directly conflicts with the institutional authority one has accepted, and a choice must be made between them. But to stand against an institution, particularly one whose authority one has wholeheartedly acknowledged, can seem an act of fearful hubris. Yet not to protest may result in a debilitating kind of self-betrayal. In this situation the individual has three options: 1) to abandon the institution and cease to identify himself with it; 2) to forge a new relationship with the institution based on a different interpretation of its dogmas and requirements; or 3) to subordinate himself to it.

Abandonment is a radical act, like amputation. Our institutional identities are deeply rooted. It is difficult to sustain either physical or spiritual life without their help; hence society generates new institutions when old ones crumble. Institutions give us the common language and body of experience that bolster us with a shared past and locate us in the world. Often a person who abandons one institution takes refuge in another, adopting its rhetoric and values as replacements. In this way art, literature, and the academy have often come to replace institutional religion.

Christa Wolf presents one aspect of the conflict between individual and institution in *A Model Childhood*, a searching inquiry into her relationship to Nazism from which she wishes, in her maturity, to disengage entirely. She wonders how deeply rooted are the attitudes it formed in her. To what extent, she asks, am I shaped by those youthful influences? How do I become free of them? How do I claim enough authority to challenge those external authorities I once invested with so much power?

Wolf recalls that an early moment of separation came for her when she maintained silence rather than report a Communist family. Only a child at the time, she knew that silence was culpable: "Nelly kept the story to herself, although she didn't forget it. She felt uneasy. Communists were people whom SA men knocked down in the streets or mowed down with sniper bullets" (52). In her autobiography she traces the long path from that silent act of defiance to her realization of the evils of Nazism and complete rejection of it. For her, growing up was a process of reeducation and gradual disengagement from the powerful early influences of unarticulated terrors, unexamined prejudices, and the voice of the Fuehrer.

Self-subordination to an institution comes either from fear of punishment or isolation, or from a considered decision to validate an external authority rather than one's own perceptions when the two conflict. Lewis's crisis of faith resulted in this kind of decision--not an irresponsible one, but a thoughtful measuring of his won potential for error against the system of beliefs he had accepted:

> Five senses; an incurably abstract intellect; a haphazardly selective memory; a set of preconceptions and assumptions so numerous that I can never examine more than a minority of them--never become even

> conscious of them all. How much of total reality can such an apparatus let through? (74-5)

Lewis sees Christianity as a corrective to the blind spots and biases in his own character. The church, he believes, with its long tradition and the amassed wisdom of ages, offers a deeper and broader perspective than is possible to any individual. In *A Grief Observed*, he therefore writes out his doubts in order to find a way back into a stronger faith than the one shaken by grief. He chooses to accept the voice of the community as an acknowledgement of his own limitations, even that of skepticism. In his last notebook he writes,

> When I lay these questions before God I get no answer. But a rather special sort of 'No answer.' It is not the locked door. It is more like a silent, certainly not uncompassionate, gaze. As though He shook His head not in refusal but waiving the question. Like, 'Peace, child; you don't understand.' (80-81)

Although he retains his identification with Christianity, Lewis must reinterpret that bond in order to maintain it. The writing in *A Grief Observed* is an act of redefintion, healing the breach that has grown between private experience and publicly confessed faith.

Autobiography is another way of accomplishing that kind of realignment with tradition. Autobiographies are often efforts to redefine one's relationship to an institution and, in some cases, to redefine the institution itself. Individual change thus is completed in a public and political act: telling one's own story can become an indictment of the institution and a proposal for reform.

Rich claims that the "institution" of motherhood "aims at ensuring that [the potential relationship of a woman to her children] shall remain under male control" (xv). "This institution," she writes, "has been a keystone of the most diverse social and political systems" (xv). Her objective in writing about crises in her own life is to demonstrate how the mythology of motherhood has fettered and entrapped women, and barred them from their most basic perceptions and feelings.

Autobiographies like this are diagnostic tools for the community; the defects of institutions become apparent in the stories of individuals within them. Change and healing begin in such diagnoses. An individual who returns from the margins affects the entire community, becomes either pariah or example, a sign of contradiction, a measure by which the community must assess itself and its assumptions and standards. But how does one learn to reclaim one's own perceptions and validate them even in defiance of the legitimating authorities one has learned to accept? The problem is a large one: we are not, most of us, voices crying in the wilderness. We need sustenance and validation from without. We need not only to turn inward and attend to our own perceptions, but also to find or create and institutionalize some larger network of support that will validate our vision of reality.

Literature is an institution that serves this function. In our time, literature has, for many, replaced religious institutions that have failed to support radically changing world views. Like the Church, it can become a source of identity and validation. Self-identification for a writer involves self-identification *as* a writer. Literary history bears out Berger's description of the dialectical evolution of all social institutions: though they are human products, they continuously act back upon those that produce them. Literary tradition, in its turn, becomes the antagonist in the writer's struggle to define his own identity. Literary conventions become ritual barriers that he must break down and rebuild to accomodate changing consciousness. Adrienne Rich introduces *Of Woman Born* with an acknowledgement that she is deliberately breaking conventions in the book: "This is in some ways a vulnerable book. I have invaded various professional domains, broken various taboos. I have used the scholarship available to me where I found it suggestive without pretending to make myself into a specialist" (xviii). Her declaration of limitation here is also a claiming of authority to alter literary and scholarly conventions.

Writers often handle the institutional aspect of literature by attempting to de-institutionalize it. Autobiography lends itself particularly well to this purpose because of its tendency to merge forms and genres, breaking down literary categories and throwing accepted rules into question. As Harold Bloom points out, every writer has to define his place in the institution of literature either by acquiescing to its prescriptions, by defying them, or by "swerving" and bending its contours to his individual needs. The last is the act of authority by which every real individual talent has finally to enter the tradition.

Connecting Tissue: Language, Story, Myth

In the body, tissue is always repairing itself: cells die and are replaced. Life is a process of constant renewal, in the social body as well as the human body. The tissue that binds us is our shared language, our common stories and myths. Languages, George Steiner writes, "are living organisms. Infinitely complex, but organisms, nevertheless. They have in them a certain life-force, and certain powers of absorption and growth. But they can decay and they can die."22 The stories we weave with our shared words are likewise living things, always in need of revision and renewal.

When language fails, as it often does in times of extremity, its revitalization requires finding new ways to use it, pruning out words that have become corrupt or inapplicable, and replacing them with terms not dulled with usage. When language ceases to engender consciousness, it has begun to die. As expressions outlive the situations that gave them particular meaning they cease to be a means of explaining the world and become part of that which needs to be explained: they separate rather than connect. Wolf wryly recalls her daughter's interpolations in discussions of the war years: "What does 'lay over' mean? says Lenka. What does 'deployed' mean?" (294)--realizing that to define those terms means trying to communicate a whole set of circumstances, a whole mentality, a spiritual atmosphere infinitely complicated and virtually incommunicable.

Wolf pauses at numerous points in her narrative to consider the impact of words laden with personal and historical associations, that seem to isolate her within the boundaries of her own memories and her own period in history. She wonders how to use such language to make her experience understandable to those for whom the word has no such resonance. Yet by explaining how words whose meanings have become specialized no longer serve to communicate, Wolf communicates most effectively the plight of individuals in Hitler's Germany as national perversity permanently altered language. To read *A Model Childhood*, is to see that the first step toward regaining a common, usable language is to acknowledge the inadequacies of an existing vocabulary. The search for words becomes a deliberate and painstaking effort to winnow out the chaff of useless, overladen, and obsolete terms. Healing the social breaches caused by the corruption of language is part of the task she sets herself.

Autobiographers of crisis often examine particular words with lapidary care, as though recovery depended upon proper definitions. And indeed it often does. Our philosophies comprise the definitions of terms that describe our lives. Lewis cut to the heart of his doubts by reconsidering what he meant by "good"--the simplest term in his moral vocabulary, and one of the hardest to define. "What reason have we," he asks, "except our own desperate wishes, to believe that God is, by any standard we can conceive, 'good'?" (33-4) What ensues is at first a theological argument, but eventually a semantic one: the problem is that any "standard we can conceive" may be the wrong standard. A deep insecurity surfaces here--a nightmare of potential isolation: what if our words do not, in fact, bear any relation to reality? What if we all use them, like the Mad Hatter, to mean "precisely what we intend them to mean, and nothing else"? We cannot assume that because we are using the same words we are necessarily describing the same things. That state of affairs prevailed in the Hitler era, when language was crippled for generations to come. Steiner describes the process of the linguistic breakdown as a slowing of natural processes:

> Actions of the mind that were once spontaneous become mechanical, frozen habits (dead metaphors, stock similes, slogans). Words grow longer and more ambiguous. Instead of style, there is rhetoric. Instead of precise common usage, there is jargon. . . . the language no longer sharpens thought but blurs it. . . . In short, the language is no longer lived; it is merely spoken.[23]

In such an environment the writer's task is reclamation.

When the terms of common speech comfortably convey similar meanings to all using them, language creates and reinforces real community. Conversely, specialized or eccentric uses of language create confusion and alienation. Sometimes, however, deliberately slanted use of words can result in an expansion of consciousness. Writers like Wolf use words idiosyncratically to make readers aware of the values those words bear, and to invite them to participate in renewing the language by consciously redefining terms.

An autobiographer always has to deal not only with the social, but with the personal value of the words he or she uses. He must claim them as his own; he must speak the language he lives. If his experiences have something universal in them, the words he uses will resonate for others, acquiring clarity and value through the "passionate intensity" that comes from claiming them in an intensely personal way.

Choosing words to describe the critical times in their lives, these writers ask themselves, do these words have the same meaning for me now as they did before? Do they mean to others what they mean to me? What kind of power do they have? How do I rid them of useless accretions and renew their power to communicate?

Just as a common language binds us together, so also the stories we tell constitute a shared body of experience that creates community. We all have stories. Telling them is a means of creating relationship--the way we sink roots in one another's lives: the answer to the question, "Who are you?" is a story. But our stories are always changing. Like words, they are living things. Continually, as we grow and change, our stories need revision. The relationships they forge likewise need to be renewed by retellings.

In the first chapter of *Of Woman Born*, Rich describes the intense sense of community generated among women telling their personal stories to one another. The experience of hearing another human being describe deep emotions--fears, angers, frustrations--is often, she finds, one of intense recognition and kinship. She describes a conversation among women about one woman's tragic story that had appeared in the newspaper, recalling,

> Every woman in that room . . . could identify with her. We spoke of the wells of anger that her story cleft open in us. . . . We spoke in the sometimes tentative, sometimes rising, sometimes bitterly witty, unrhetorical tones and language of women who had met together over our common work, poetry, and who found another common ground in an unacceptable, but

> undeniable anger. The words are being spoken now, are being written down . . . (5)

Women weaving the threads of their individual stories together, like women at a quilting frame, produce a communal product of great complexity and beauty, its whole greater than its parts. They produce, as well, a network on intense relationships. Finding the language for those stories, as Rich describes it, is a process of breaking up the web of language and reweaving it into a stronger fabric. Autobiography among women has become something of a collective activity, an oral tradition through which a new female mythology is beginning to take shape. Through autobiography in its many forms, we teach one another how to live. Life stories set precedents and standards; we measure ourselves by one another. We live and move and have our being in relationship to others, and those relationship are forged by the stories we tell.

Every autobiography is a way--a map--a trail blazed in the wilderness of human experience that serves to remind the reader that someone has been this way before. To someone lost in that wilderness, the sight of a blaze is an immense comfort. Through autobiography we have a way to heal not only ourselves, but one another.

Audiences

"This is my letter to the world," Emily Dickinson wrote. Most autobiographers might well preface their works in the same way. As they heal themselves, they also repair the links that connect them with society--necessary even to a recluse like Dickinson. Every writer writes from within a relationship and creates a series of relationships by writing. The laying on of hands in ancient healing rituals is symbolically replicated in the words we use to reach out to touch one another. By means of those words we establish our kinship and reinstate ourselves in the body of society, the whole of which we are parts. The ability to enter into relationships is one of the signs of healing; the aim of any act of healing is not only internal harmony, but the ability to function in the world at large, and to maintain both individuality and connection. Autobiography is an act that ripples outward from the individual life to successively larger audiences. At each level of reception it can serve a healing function.

The autobiographer's first audience is himself. The written page is his mirror. In that dialogue he discovers a self that comes into being in the act of writing. The contents of the unconscious may first appear there in a form that allows them to be recognized and dealt with.

Usually there is, beyond the self, an intimate audience for whom the autobiography is written--the author's children or family. Sometimes that audience is dead, and the autobiography is an act of commemoration--as Wiesel claims, for instance, that *Night* is his *Kaddish* for his father. Then there is the wider community to whom the autobiography is addressed: Jews in Wiesel's case, Christians in Lewis's, women in Rich's.

Ultimately, an autobiography is a letter to the world. There is something in any human life for everyone. An autobiography is a reminder that no suffering, no humiliation, no joy, no idiosyncrasy or angle of vision is too alien to be recognized as one more of life's possibilities.

The ripples widen. Autobiography reiterates, reinforces, and deepens the truths we have discovered about our lives. It demonstrates the endless potential for transformation that language can work magically upon experience. The story is a sign of hope, for we do "live by stories." As an art form, autobiography is interesting in its own right for the aesthetic problems it introduces, for its tendency to break down and reform our expectations, and for its flexibility as a literary tool. It illustrates the possibilities of formal eclecticism, and forms a nexus between art and life that forces a critical reader continually to question his assumptions about that relationship.

But a good autobiography will always be of more than literary interest to a sensitive reader. Even the most sophisticated reader, who recognizes the deceptive overlap between truth and fiction, must be touched in a particular way by "true stories." When a child asks, "Is this a true story?" he wants to know because it makes a difference. As autobiography engenders self-confrontation in the writer, so it also brings a reader face to face with his or her own humanity. For both writer and reader it is an instrument not only of self-evaluation and of connection, but also of revision and growth. We need to hear one another's stories, and we need to tell our own, because, being human, we need to be healed.

1 Ezrahi, p. 79.

2 Albert Gelpi, essay in Gelpi, p. 141.

3 Merleau-Ponty, quoted in Ezrahi, p. 68.

4 Cargas, p. 6.

5 Rainer Maria Rilke, *Letters to a Young Poet*, trans. M.D. Herter (New York: W.W. Norton & Co., 1962), p. 59.

6 Cargas, p. 6.

7 Cargas, p. 8.

8 Cargas, p. 33.

9 Cargas, p. 110.

10 Cargas, p. 98.

11 Janet Varner Gunn, p. 62.

12 Steiner, p. 141.

13 Michel Foucault, "What is an Author?" *Partisan Review* 42 (1975), pp. 149ff.

14 Jung, *Memories* , p. 14.

15 Peter Berger, *The Sacred Canopy* (New York: Doubleday, Anchor Books, 1969), p. 13.

16 Gunn, p. 31.

17 Estelle Jelinek, ed., *Women's Autobiography* (Bloomington: Indiana University Press, 1980), p. 52.

18 Spacks, p. 33.

[19] Ezrahi, p. 218.

[20] Berger, p. 3.

[21] Berger, p. 37.

[22] Steiner, p. 96.

[23] Steiner, p. 96.

BIBLIOGRAPHY

Adams, Henry. *The Education of Henry Adams.* Boston: Houghton, Mifflin Co., 1961.

Ahlstrom, Sydney E. *A Religious History of the American People.* New Haven: Yale University Press, 1972.

Alvarez, A. *The Savage God: A Study of Suicide.* New York: Bantam, 1972.

Arana, R. Victoria. "Elegant Intimacy: Monologue and Dialogue in Post-World War I Autobiography." Paper presented at the 1983 convention of the Modern Language Association, New York.

Berenbaum, Michael. *The Vision of the Void: Theological Reflections on the Works of Elie Wiesel.* Middletown, CN: Wesleyan University Press, 1979.

Berger, Peter. *The Sacred Canopy.* New York: Doubleday, Anchor Books, 1969.

Bettelheim, Bruno. *Surviving and Other Essays.* New York: Vintage Books, 1979.

Bloch, Chana. *The Secrets of the Tribe.* New York: The Sheep Meadow Press, 1980.

Brittain, Vera. *Chronicle of Youth: War Diary, 1913-1917.* London: Victor Gollancz, Ltd., 1981.

----------. *Testament of Experience.* London: Virago, Ltd., 1981.

----------. *Testament of Friendship.* London: Virago, Ltd., 1978.

----------. *Testament of Youth* . London: Virago, Ltd., 1978.

Bruss, Elizabeth. *Autobiographical Acts: The Changing Situation of a Literary Genre* . Baltimore: Johns Hopkins University Press, 1976.

Burke, Kenneth. *Counter-Statement.* Berkeley: University of California Press, 1968.

----------. *Language as Symbolic Action.* Berkeley: University of California Press, 1966.

----------. *The Philosophy of Literary Form.* Berkeley: University of California Press, 1973.

Cargas, Harry James. *Harry James Cargas in Converstion with Elie Wiesel.* New York: Paulist Press, 1976.

Church, Richard. "The Art of Autobiography." *Cornhill* 171 (1960-61) 469-480.

Conroy, Frank. *Stop-Time* (New York: Penguin Books, 1967), p. 21.

Corsini, Raymond, ed. *Current Psychotherapies.* Itasca, IL: F.E. Peacock Publishing, Inc., 1973.

Couser, Thomas. "Of Time and Identity: Walt Whitman and Gertrude Stein as Autobiographers." *Texas Studies in Litrature and Language*, 17 (1975-6) 787-804.

----------. "The Shape of Death in American Autobiography." *Hudson Review* 31 (1978) 53-66.

----------. *American Autobiography: The Prophetic Mode.* Amherst: University of Massachusetts Press, 1979.

Cox, James. "Autobiography and America." *Virginia Quarterly Review* , 47 (1971) 252-277.

Culler, Jonathan. *Structuralist Poetics: Structuralism, Linguistics and the Study of Literature*. Ithaca: Cornell University Press, 1975.

Daly, Mary. *Beyond God the Father: Toward a Philosophy of Women's Liberation*. Boston: Beacon Press, 1973.

Des Pres, Terrence. *The Survivor: An Anatomy of Life in the Death Camps*. New York: Simon and Schuster, Pocket Books, 1977.

Earle, William. *The Autobiographical Consciousness*. Chicago: Quadrangle Books, 1972.

Elsbree, Langdon. *The Rituals of Life: Patterns in Narratives*. Port Washington, NY: National University Publications, 1982.

Empson, William. *Some Versions of Pastoral*. Norfolk, CN: New Directions Books, 1960), p. 23.

Ezrahi, Sidra D. *By Words Alone: The Holocaust in Literature*. Chicago: University of Chicago Press, 1980.

Feder, Elaine and Bernard. *The Expressive Arts Therapies*. Englewood Cliffs, NJ: Prentice-Hall, Inc., 1981.

Ferguson, Marilyn. *The Aquarian Conspiracy: Personal and Social Transformation in the 1980's*. Los Angeles: J.P. Tarcher, Inc., 1980.

Foucault, Michel. "What is an Author?" *Partisan Review* 42 (1975) 603-14.

Frankl, Viktor. *Man's Search for Meaning*. New York: Washington Square Press, 1963.

Friedman, Susan. "Theories of Autobiography and Modernist Self-Creations in H.D.'s Canon." Paper presented at the 1983 convention of the Modern Language Association, New York.

Frisch, Max. *Montauk* . Trans. Geoffrey Skelton. New York: Harcourt, Brace, Jovanovich, 1976.

Fussell, Paul. *The Great War and Modern Memory*. London: Oxford University Press, 1971.

Gelpi, Barbara and Albert. *Adrienne Rich's Poems*. New York: W.W. Norton and Co., 1975.

Gilligan, Carol. *In a Different Voice*. Cambridge, MA: Harvard University Press, 1982.

Goleman, Daniel and Kathleen R. Speeth, eds. *The Essential Psychotherapies*. New York: New American Library, 1982.

Gray, Rockwell. "Time Present and Time Past: The Ground of Autobiography." *Soundings* 64 (1) 52-94.

Green, Roger L. and Walter Hooper. *C.S. Lewis: A Biography*. New York: Harcourt, Brace, Jovanovich, 1974.

Gregg, Lee, and Erwin R. Steinberg, eds. *Cognitive Processes in Writing*. Hillsdale, NJ: Lawrence Erlbaum Associates, Publishers, 1980.

Greif, Hans-Juergen. *Christa Wolf: "Wie Sind Wir So Geworden Wie Wir Heute Sind?"* Bern: Peter Lang, 1978.

Gunn, Janet Varner. *Autobiography: Toward a Poetics of Experience* . Philadelphia: University of Pennsylvania Press, 1982.

Handke, Peter. *A Sorrow Beyond Dreams*. Trans. Ralph Mannheim. New York: Farrar, Straus and Giroux, 1974.

----------. *Wunschloses Unglueck: Erzaehlung*. Salzburg: Residenz Verlag, 1972.

Hart, Francis. "Notes for an Anatomy of Modern Autobiography." *New Literary History* 1 (1970) 485-511.

Hartman, Geoffrey. *Criticism in the Wilderness.* New Haven: Yale University Press, 1980.

Hassan, Ihab. *The Literature of Silence.* New York: Alfred A.Knopf, 1967.

Hoggart, Richard. "A Question of Tone: Some Problems in Autobiographical Writing." *Critical Quarterly* 5 (1963) 73-90.

Jelinek, Estelle, ed. *Women's Autobiography.* Bloomington: University of Indiana Press, 1980.

Jung, Carl G. *Aion: Researches into the Phenomenology of the Self.* Princeton: Princeton University Press, 1959.

----------. *The Basic Writings of C.G. Jung.* Ed. Violet de Laszlo. New York: Random House, The Modern Library, 1959.

----------. *Man and His Symbols.* New York: Doubleday, 1964.

----------. *Memories, Dreams and Reflections.* Trans. Richard and Clara Winston. New York: Random House, 1963.

----------. *Modern Man in Search of a Soul.* New York: Harcourt, Brace, World, 1933.

----------. *Psyche and Symbol.* Ed. Violet de Laszlo. New York: Harcourt, Brace, World, 1933.

----------. *The Undiscovered Self.* New York: New American Library, 1958.

Kermode, Frank. *The Sense of an Ending: Studies in the Theory of Fiction.* New York: Oxford University Press, 1967.

Kubler-Ross, Elizabeth. *On Death and Dying*. New York: Macmillan, 1969.

Kuhn, Thomas. *The Structure of Scientific Revolutions*. Chicago: University of Chicago Press, 1962.

Laing, R.D. *The Divided Self*. Harmondsworth, England: Penguin Books, 1969.

Langer, Lawrence. *The Holocaust and the Literary Imagination*. New Haven: Yale University Press, 1975.

----------. *Versions of Survival: The Holocaust and the Human Spirit*. Albany: State University of New York Press, 1982.

Lewis, C.S. *A Grief Observed*. New York: Bantam Books, 1980.

----------. *Letters of C.S. Lewis*. W.H. Lewis, ed. New York: Harcourt, Brace and World, Inc., 1966.

----------. *Surprised by Joy: The Shape of My Early Life*. New York: Harcourt, Brace and Co., 1955.

Lloyd, Robert A. *Images of Survival*. New York: Dodd, Mead and Co., 1973.

Mandel, Barrett J. "The Past in Autobiography." *Soundings* 64 (1) 52-74.

Marcus, Laura. "Autobiography and Psychoanalysis." Paper presented at the 1983 convention of the Modern Language Association, New York.

McConnell, J. *The Shattered Self: The Psychological and Religious Search for Selfhood*. Philadelphia: Pilgrim Press, 1971.

Miller, Casey and Kate Swift. *Words and Women*. New York: Doubleday, Anchor Books, 1977.

Mitchell, W.J.T., ed. *On Narrative*. Chicago: University of Chicago Press, 1981.

Munsat, Stanley. *The Concept of Memory* . New York: Random House, 1967.

Murray, Donald. *Learning Through Teaching*. Montclair, NJ: Boynton/Cook Publishers, 1983.

Neumann, Bernd. *Identitaet und Rollenzwang*. Frankfurt: Athenaeum Verlag, 1970.

Olney, James, ed. *Autobiography: Essays Theoretical and Critical*. Princeton: Princeton University Press, 1980.

----------. *Metaphors of Self: The Meaning of Autobiography*. Princeton: Princeton University Press, 1980.

Pachter, Marc. *Telling Lives: The Biographer's Art*. Washington, D.C.: New Republic Books, 1979.

Pascal, Roy. *Design and Truth in Autobiography*. Cambridge,MA: Harvard University Press, 1960.

Pike, Burton. "Time in Autobiography." *Comparative Literature* 28 (1976) 326-42.

Pilling, John. *Autobiography and Imagination: Studies in Self-Scrutiny*. London: Routledge and Kegan Paul, 1981.

Pirsig, Robert. *Zen and the Art of Motorcycle Maintenance: An Inquiry into Values*. New York: Bantam Books, 1974.

Progoff, Ira. *At a Journal Workshop*. New York: Dialogue House Library, 1975.

----------. *The Symbolic and the Real*. New York: Julian Press, Inc., 1963.

Rich, Adrienne. *Adrienne Rich's Poems.* Ed. Albert and Barbara Gelpi. New York: W.W. Norton and Co., 1975.

----------. *On Lies, Secrets, and Silence: Selected Prose, 1966-1978.* New York: W.W. Norton and Co., 1979.

----------. *Of Woman Born: Motherhood as Experience and Institution.* New York: Bantam Books, 1976.

----------. *Poems: Selected and New 1950-1974.* New York: W.W. Norton and Co., 1975.

Riquelme, J.P. "The Unspeakable 'I' of Modernism: From Yeats to Beckett." Paper presented at the 1983 convention of the Modern Language Association, New York.

Rilke, Rainer Maria. *Letters to a Young Poet.* Trans. M.D. Herter. New York: W.W. Norton and Co., 1962.

Sauer, Klaus. *Christa Wolf: Materialenbuch.* Darmstadt: Lucherhand, 1979.

Shapiro, Stephen. "The Dark Continent of Literature: Autobiography." *Comparative Literature Studies* 5 (1968) 421-454.

Shuman, Edwin. *How to Judge a Book: A Handy Method of Criticism for the General Reader.* Boston: Houghton, Mifflin Co., 1910.

Simon, Neil. "Portrait of the Writer as Schizophrenic" in *Collected Plays of Neil Simon.* New York: Random House, 1971.

Spacks, Patricia Meyer. "Women's Stories, Women's Selves." *The Hudson Review* 30 (1977) 29-46.

Spengemann, William C. *The Forms of Autobiography: Episodes in the History of a Literary Genre*. New Haven: Yale University Press, 1980.

Steiner, George. *Language and Silence*. New York: Athenaeum, 1982.

Stephan, Alexander. *Christa Wolf*. Munich: Beck Verlag, 1979.

Stone, Albert. *The American Autobiography*. Englewood Cliffs, NJ: Prentice-Hall, Inc., 1981.

----------. *Autobiographical Occasions and Original Acts: Versions of American Identity from Henry Adams to Nate Shaw*. Philadelphia: University of Pennsylvania Press, 1982.

Strauss, Anselm L. *Mirrors and Masks: The Search for Identity*. University of California at San Francisco: The Sociology Press, 1969.

Sturrock, John. "The New Model Autobiographer." *New Literary History*, 9 (1977) 51-63.

Wiesel, Elie. *Legends of Our Time*. Trans. Marion Wiesel. New York: Avon Books, 1968.

----------. *Night*. Trans. Stella Rodway. New York: Bantam Books, 1960.

Wolf, Christa. *A Model Childhood*. Trans. Ursule Molinaro and Hedwig Rappolt. New York: Farrar, Straus and Giroux, 1980.

----------. *Kindheitsmuster*. Darmstadt: Luchterhand, Gmbh., 1979.

----------. *Lesen und Schreiben: Aussaetze und Betrachtungen*. Berlin: Aufbau Verlag, 1973.

----------. *The Reader and the Writer: Essays, Sketches, Memories*. New York: International Publishers, 1977.

Young, T.R. *New Sources of Self.* New York: Pergamon Press, Inc., 1972.